3rd hist

398

D0754417

e

෨෨෨෨෨෨

DRUMS AND TRUMPETS

෨෨෨෨෨෨

THE MIRROR OF BRITAIN SERIES

General Editor : Kevin Crossley-Holland

DRUMS AND TRUMPETS

THE HOUSE OF STUART

Kirsty McLeod

ANDRE DEUTSCH

First published 1977 by
André Deutsch Limited
105 Great Russell Street London WC1

Printed Offset Litho in Great Britain by
Cox and Wyman Ltd
London, Fakenham and Reading

Colour plates printed by
Raithby Lawrence, Leicester

ISBN 0 233 96861 X

For my two nieces, Lucy and Georgina

இஇஇஇஇஇ

ACKNOWLEDGMENTS

இஇஇஇஇஇ

Acknowledgments are due to the following for permission to reproduce the colour and black and white plates: The Warden and Fellows of All Souls College, Oxford, 51; The British Library Board, 7, 23; The Trustees of the British Museum 3, 7, 20, 46; The Courtauld Institute of Art, 5, 56; Department of the Environment, Crown Copyright, 3; John R. Freeman & Co., 12, 1, 4, 40, 61; Angelo Hornak, 5, 11, 17, 27, 53, 54; A. F. Kersting, 55; The Mansell Collection, 2, 13, 15, 16, 22, 24, 25, 26, 28, 29, 37, 38, 41, 44, 45, 59; Mary Evans Picture Library, 6, 8, 12, 14, 18, 19, 30, 31, 32, 33, 42; The National Monuments Record, Crown Copyright, 39, 57, 58; The National Portrait Gallery, 1, 2, 4, 8, 9, 9, 21, 34, 35(b), 36, 43; The National Trust, 60; HM The Queen, 6, 35(a); The Royal Institute of British Architects, 52; The Society of Antiquaries, 47, 50; The Duke of Buccleugh, Victoria and Albert Museum, 35(c), 35(d); The Trustees of the Victoria and Albert Museum, 10, 11; Wayland Picture Library, 10, 48, 49.

Thanks are also due to Caroline Bingham for reading the manuscript and making helpful suggestions, and to Ruth Crossley-Holland for her invaluable picture research.

CONTENTS

Introduction	9
COURTLY LIFE (1603–40)	11
James I (1603–25)	11
Charles I (1625–49)	16
COUNTRY LIFE (1603–40)	25
The Country Gentry	25
The Clergy	37
The Yeomen and Farm Labourers	42
TOWN LIFE (1603–40)	48
London	49
THE GROWTH OF PURITANISM	60
The Puritan Religion	60
Puritans and Parliament	63
Puritans in the New World	64
The Influence of Puritanism on Thought	68
CIVIL WAR (1640–49)	70
THE COMMONWEALTH (1649–60)	78

Life after the Restoration   86
The Courts:
  Charles II (1660–85)   86
  James II (1685–8)   94
  William (1689–1702) and Mary (1689–94)   99
  Anne (1702–14)   108
Town Life   112
Country Life   134

Bibliography   138
Index   141

INTRODUCTION

W H E N we read in history books about the French Revolution or the Russian Revolution it is natural for us to ask ourselves how England managed to escape the same kind of violent upheaval. To find the answer we have to go back to the seventeenth century when the Stuarts were on the throne. The long struggles between King and Parliament ended by securing our liberties without destroying the whole fabric of our society.

In England there is still a monarchy because Crown and Parliament, having fought each other, learnt to compromise. It was the spirit of unity and tolerance displayed by both sides after the Civil War that laid the foundations of the English parliamentary democracy, the way the country is governed now, with a choice of parties and a free vote. England has one of the most ancient and stable democracies in the world and for this the English owe direct thanks to their ancestors and the compromise they worked out in the seventeenth century.

The English owe the seventeenth century much more besides: their freedom of speech – the right to think and say what they like about whom they like, no matter how important they are; their freedom of worship, so that they can go to whichever church they like or not go at all if they choose; the whole moderate, tolerant tone that is the hallmark of the English way of life with its emphasis on the liberty of conscience of the individual. All of these were first established in the seventeenth century.

The seeds of the conflict which erupted in the seventeenth century had been sown in the century before when Henry VIII

high-handedly broke with Rome and the Catholic church to form
an English church which owed allegiance to the English monarch
rather than the Pope. To devout Catholics this was heresy and
could not be stomached. When Elizabeth I tried to heal the rift
and create a moderate national Church of England, she was bound
to fail. To the Catholics the head of the church had to be the
papal father in Rome. To the suspicious Protestants, anyone
owing allegiance to a foreign power was an outsider, possibly even
a traitor. The most extreme of the Protestants were the fiercely
patriotic, anti-Catholic Puritans, intent on 'purifying' the church
of Roman ceremony and pomp. With such differences of opinion
among her subjects, how could Elizabeth hope for unity? Yet the
strange thing was that the conflict, when it came, paved the way
for just the unity it had appeared to destroy. When the fighting
was over, every man was prepared to respect his neighbour's
right to his own beliefs and his own forms of worship. And so it
has remained.

But we have to remember that seventeenth-century England
was more than a battleground for liberties. It was the century of
Shakespeare and Milton, of Pepys and Newton and Christopher
Wren. Wren's masterpiece is St Paul's Cathedral and when we go
into it today and look around at the elegant craftsmanship and
confident, soaring architecture, we are reminded that in the arts
as well as in politics and religion, Stuart England has left us a
wonderful legacy.

🔢🔢🔢🔢🔢

COURTLY LIFE

🔢🔢🔢🔢🔢

JAMES I (1603–25)

A TRAVELLER journeying north in the late spring of 1603 might well have passed on the road a large, straggling and ill-assorted procession. If he had looked closely and known what to look for, he might have discerned among the travel-weary Scots nobles, English well-wishers and the hangers-on who accompanied them, the tall, gangling figure of his new king. James I and VI (see colour plate 1), at the age of thirty-seven, King of England *and* Scotland, cousin to the late Queen Elizabeth and great-great-grandson of Henry VII, would not have stood out in such a company. For a monarch, he was deliberately homely and simple in his dress. Any elegance that he might have had was spoiled by the bulky outline of the heavy, quilted doublet he wore to protect him from stiletto attacks.

And in any case James I and VI was far from elegant. In time his affectation of simplicity was to give way to unashamed sloven-liness. He was tall, clumsy, loose-limbed, shambling, 'his fingers,' as a contemporary noted, 'ever . . . fidling about his codpiece' as he walked. He slurred his speech, slobbered over his drink and shocked many of the English courtiers with his crudely anatomical sense of humour.

But for the moment the members of the Privy Council who came out thirteen miles from London to greet James were well satisfied with what they saw. The new king had a quick, incisive mind. His reputation for decisiveness and determination had preceded him. After the endless bickering between factions which

1. The Great Hall at Theobalds, home of the Cecil family.

had marred the closing years of Elizabeth's reign, it was enough. They could afford to smile indulgently at James's boast that he was 'an old, experienced King, needing no lessons'. Nevertheless, anyone of foresight who had scrutinized the king's progress through England must have seen the warning signs. James's watery blue eyes glittered at the sight of so much peaceful richness; his slack jaw hung open as he saw the great houses of his lords. Burghley and Theobalds (see plate 1), the two great houses of the Cecil family which he visited, must have been a revelation, with their endless halls and dazzling vistas, to this poverty-stricken monarch who had once boasted only two or three jewels and less than £100 worth of plate in his coffer.

No wonder that, used as he was to the bare stone walls of Holy-rood Palace in Edinburgh, James revelled in the luxury of Whitehall, his great white palace beside the Thames. For luxury it was. The Jacobean court, like its Elizabethan predecessor, housed over 1000 courtiers, government officers, retainers and servants. All under one roof, they revolved around one common centre and purpose – the person of the king.

Presiding over this enormous work force were the two highest officers at court – the Lord Chamberlain, responsible for the 'upstairs' domain, and the Lord Steward, in charge of such 'downstairs' duties as provisioning and housekeeping. 'Upstairs' included all those who came in daily contact with the king. Mostly, like the grooms, pages, cup-bearers and messengers, they were relegated to the Outer Chamber. The Privy Chamber with its smaller staff was for the king's use when he desired seclusion. The Bedchamber was even more exclusive: an inner group of James's personal servants and intimate friends. But the Lord Chamberlain also had under his jurisdiction the seven permanent departments at court – the offices of the Great Wardrobe, Revels, Tents and Toils, Armoury, Works, the Ordnance and the Mint. He controlled the Chapel Royal with its staff of twenty-three gentlemen besides the clergy; the musicians and their necessary accompaniment, the instrument-makers; the Masters of Otter Hounds, Harthounds, Harriers and Hawking, and the nine-strong medical staff who guarded the king's health.

But this was only part of the work force. In addition, Whitehall employed a vast, unseen army, presided over at a remote distance by the Lord Steward, who cooked and washed and cleaned. The Kitchen, the Pantry, the Buttery, the Spicery, the Poultery, the Confectionery, the Scalding-House – they were all necessary in a court where the king and queen alone sat down to twenty-four-course meals, or thirty courses on state occasions.

With such prodigal consumption – 1400 lambs and 3000 beef carcasses a year, on average – the opportunities for corruption were immense, despite the efforts of the Knight Marshal whose job it was to police the court. Yet in a way, the lower orders who cheated the king were only aping their lords and masters. The courtiers, too, expected to live off the Crown's bounty. Apart from grants of cash, King James had at his disposal numerous lucrative court posts and sinecures which he could award to a deserving courtier. The Master of the Wardrobe, for example, an ambitious baronet from Scotland, made his fortune selling off the late queen's thousands of dresses. And the small, vellum-bound *Books of Offices* which listed the court appointments and their fees were in greater demand than a modern bestseller. Nor was it the greedy or the opportunists only who scanned them. The spectre of impoverishment haunted many of those in attendance at James's court. The king had been starved of wealth for so long that he wanted to see it perpetually around him. No courtier dared venture outside his door unless he were dressed with as much magnificence as he could afford. 'When your posterity shall see our pictures,' commented Richard Rowlands with some truth in 1605, 'they shall think we are foolishly proud of apparel.' With the establishment of blonde, giddy Anne of Denmark, James's queen, at Denmark House, the women, too, entered the lists. It became the custom at court after each night's glittering entertainment to guess the value of the fortune in jewels around each lady's neck. It seemed, according to the sardonic and observant playwright, Ben Jonson, that the sole duty of great personages was to look as rich and magnificent as possible.

As well as 'a dauncing queene', the courtiers had 'an huntinge kinge' to contend with. James spent a large part of the year in the saddle. Ever restless, he rode from palace to palace, hunting lodge to hunting lodge, leaving his court to struggle after him as best they could. Those of them with seats in good hunting country could count on the expensive privilege of playing host to the king. With two parks to maintain, hawks and horses to buy and 400 deer to fence in, it was no wonder the hard-pressed steward of Viscount Lisle hoped that hunting was a passing fashion. Prominent families like the Cecils found themselves singled out too often for their liking. When James wanted to entertain Christian IV of Denmark, his brother-in-law, he did so at Lord Salisbury's house and expense. A long and disapproving description of the drunken banquet at Theobalds, Salisbury's country estate, has been left to us by Sir John Harington, inventor of the water-closet. He mentions the appearance 'in rich dress' of three figures representing Faith, Hope and Charity, followed by the disappearance of Faith and Hope, 'both sick and spewing in the lower hall . . . wine did so occupy their upper chambers'. A ballad of the time contrasted such debauchery with the sober court of the previous reign. First, the old days:

With an old song made by an aged pate
Of an old gentleman that had an old estate,
Who kept an old house, at an old bountiful rate,
With an old porter to relieve poor people at his gate;
Like an old Courtier of the Queen's,
And the Queen's old Courtier.

Then, the new:

With a new flourishing gallant, new come to his land,
Who kept a brace of new painted creatures to be at his hand,
And could take up a thousand readily upon his own new bond,
And be drunk in a new tavern till he be not able to go or stand;
Like a new Courtier of the King's,
Like the King's new Courtier.

One of many nursery rhymes with historical associations mocked the king's newly rich Scottish favourites.

Hark! Hark!
The dogs do bark,
The beggars have come to town.
Some in rags,
And some in tags,
And some in velvet gowns.

The truth was that, except for a chosen few, most of the king's courtiers saw little return for the financial investment of waiting on him. Whatever favours he had to spare went not to them, nor even to his wife whom he totally neglected, but to a small and exclusive band of young bloods, headed by a handsome Scot named Robert Carr. Considering James's upbringing in an exclusively male environment, it was not surprising that he preferred the company of men. But as time passed his critics were less and less inclined to make allowances. His marked favouritism to his intimates shocked many of the old school and inflamed the jealous divisions within the court. Worse was to come. In 1614, when the chestnut-haired, effeminately beautiful George Villiers, future Duke of Buckingham (see colour plate 2) rocketed into royal favour he made Carr look like the simple Scots laird he was. The grasping Villiers family – 'I desire to advance it above all others' said James in 1618 – lost no time in seizing the richest plums at court. Their friends and relations infiltrated every aspect of government, watched complacently by the totally infatuated king. In 1617, fourteen years after the start of his reign, James sent all those on the fringe of court life – the country gentry without a town house – home. He himself, in the eight years left to him, grew more and more inaccessible, playing 'dear dad' to Buckingham his favourite, whom he regarded as his 'sweet child and wife'. His subjects, whether common people or the be-leaguered country gentry, seldom set eyes on their sovereign. When he was urged to show himself to his people in the manner of his predecessor, his reply was characteristically blunt: 'God's wounds! I will pull down my breeches and they shall also see my arse.'

As a result the country as a whole showed little grief when James died in 1625, although his son and heir, Charles, perhaps to compensate, arranged a magnificent state funeral. The sixty-year-old king was buried with more dignity than he had ever managed to display during his lifetime, when, as the French Ambassador had acidly commented about his drinking habits, his solution to every problem was 'ever the bottle'.

CHARLES I (1625–49)

James left his son a dangerous legacy. In 1625 Charles I inherited serious problems along with his kingdom. The implications for the monarchy of the isolation and unpopularity of the court party, the disaffection of the disgruntled country gentry and the growing mistrust between them were grave indeed.

As if this were not enough, Charles had other disadvantages of character and upbringing to contend with. He had lived until he was twelve in the shadow of the heir to the throne, his handsome, athletic, gifted brother, Henry. Charles by contrast was a weak, sickly child who was not expected to live long let alone succeed to the throne. Yet in 1612 when the energetic, vital Henry caught a chill, fell into a coma and died, Charles suddenly found himself thrust into the limelight as his father's heir. His grief and loneliness increased with the departure from England of his beloved sister, Elizabeth, who was married to Frederick V, Elector Palatine; and despatched to Germany. Charles never saw her again. He was left in England, the only English royal child. As a result, he grew up set apart both by his position and by his Stuart belief in the divine right of kingship. Even with those he knew well, he was never sufficiently extrovert to be natural. Charles was shy, reserved, serious and consistently ill at ease with people. He hid his discomfort behind a coldly dignified, formal mask. His people never came to know him, let alone love him and he, on his side, was totally divorced from them. When he went to the scaffold twenty-four years hence, it was as an exquisitely dressed, elegantly mannered kingly mystery, never once having

2. Three heads of Charles I, painted by Van Dyck to assist the sculptor
Bernini with a bust, since lost.

managed, or indeed tried to bridge the gulf of suspicion and mistrust which separated him from his people. No wonder the great Italian sculptor, Bernini, seeing the proud, resigned, hauntingly sad triple portrait by Van Dyck (see plate 2) pronounced the king 'doomed . . . Never have I beheld features more unfortunate . . .'

At the beginning of his reign, Charles had the added misfortune of being in thrall to Buckingham, like his father. The wily favourite had taken pains to ensure his future by captivating the heterosexual Charles as well as his homosexual father. He did it with a mixture of swagger and sycophancy. Nervous, diffident, starved of affection, Charles I hero-worshipped his dazzling courtier who, by excelling at dancing, riding, swordsmanship and conversation, represented all the things that Charles was not. 'Steenie' – so called because he resembled a miniature of St Stephen in the royal collection – brought romance and glamour into the young king's lonely life.

'Steenie' was also to be one of the causes of his downfall. More than ever, he encouraged in Charles the fatal Stuart tendency to see politics in terms of personalities. This suited Buckingham, whose hold over the king was absolute, but Charles himself became susceptible to the intrigues of court factions and increasingly unable to distinguish between opposition to his policies and treason. To be fair, there was nothing new in this. Before the growth of an official opposition party, criticism of the sovereign was always in danger of being construed as treason; the same danger had existed under Elizabeth I. But in the contemporary climate of opinion, Charles's lack of judgement, along with his inability to compromise, exasperated the growing number of his opponents. He seemed incapable of understanding that what was legally right might be politically wrong. He never mastered this failing even after Buckingham's assassination in 1628, an event which went unregretted by the majority of the populace who had seen the Villiers wax fat on the proceeds from their monopolies in the trade of gold and silver thread. Lucy Hutchinson, a contemporary, spoke for many of his subjects when she wondered how so good a man could make so bad a king.

For Charles was a good man, a religious man, honourable,

conscientious and a kind and faithful husband. After the excesses and indecencies of the last reign, Whitehall underwent a moral spring-cleaning. A decorous elegance and strict etiquette were the keynotes of the new order. Under the king's careful patronage, the arts flourished, earning him the accolade of 'most art-loving Prince in Europe'. Inspired by this, Peter Paul Rubens who came to England first of all as a Netherlands diplomat, stayed to paint the ceiling of Inigo Jones's new Banqueting House (see colour plate 3), still standing today. Jones himself, self-educated son of a Smithfield cloth-worker who rose to become Surveyor of the King's Works under James I, was largely responsible for bringing Renaissance architecture to England. At the beginning of the century he had travelled to Italy and returned full of enthusiasm for the men of the Italian Renaissance and their rediscovery of the classical architecture of Greece and Rome. As a result, his graceful, pillared classical buildings stood out among brick-and-timber Tudor London (see plate 3) as new and different and, to most of his fellow countrymen, un-English as Rubens's curved nudes and voluptuous flesh-tints were to a generation brought up on the flat portraits of the Elizabethans. In Covent Garden he even attempted a classical piazza (see plate 4), lined by uniform rows of houses and dominated by the closest he could come to a temple – a simple pillared church.

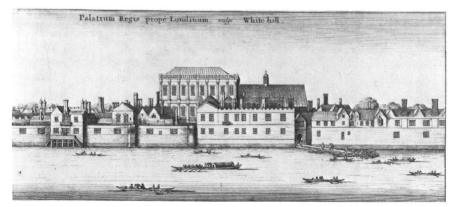

Palatium Regis prope Londinum, vulgo White-hall.

3. The Whitehall of Charles I, showing the Banqueting House in the background, all that remains now of a disastrous fire in 1698

4. Inigo Jones' classical piazza at Covent Garden with the church of
St Paul's in the centre

Somehow, all this new-fangled 'foreign' art symbolized to the
less sophisticated country gentry all they considered wrong with
the effete, extravagant, over-privileged Stuart courts. They themselves, even those who could afford not to, clung to their homely
medieval Gothic heritage and did not see why their betters should
not follow suit. It was to be a long time before classicism trickled
out into the shires. The glowing exception was in Wiltshire where
the Earl of Pembroke commissioned Jones and his deputy at the
Office of Works, John Webb, to make some additions to Wilton
House. The result was the glorious suite known as the Single and
Double Cube Rooms, where the Jacobean tradition of heavy
panelling was abandoned in favour of plain walls ornamented
with classical motifs and festooned with a riot of ornament and
carving – flowers, fruit, ribbons, palms and masks.

But among the less enlightened in the country, the murmurs of
criticism grew louder at the spectacle of the king 'squandering
away millions of pounds upon old rotten pictures and broken
nosed marbles'. It was a feeling which was to explode in one of the
tragedies of English art history – the break-up of Charles I's
magnificent art collection by Oliver Cromwell's men after the
Civil War.

It is probably true to say that had this not happened, England would own today many of the greatest pictures in the world. Indeed, the inventory of them still survives and all the most illustrious names are there – Titian, Tintoretto, Mantegna, Corregio, Raphael, Giorgione – together with busts by Bernini, antiquities and gold and silver and jewels. The pictures, which today would be priceless, raised then the paltry sum of £118,000 – only £8000 more in value than the jewels James I's queen would wear in a single night. One of the rare survivals from the sale was Raphael's cartoon, now in the National Gallery.

Charles also patronized living artists. The Dutch artist, Daniel Mytens, found a niche at his court, as did the portrait-painter, Anthony Van Dyck. In the sensibility and almost aristocratic reticence of his portraits, he had much in common with King Charles himself and indeed, he was a supreme propandist for the Royalist cause, treated almost as an equal by the king's supporters at court, as no other painter had been before him. He painted Henrietta Maria, Charles's French-born queen, her dark hair curled into the latest French fashion, christened by the wags, *tête de mouton*, 'sheep's head' (see colour plate 4).

In 1636 in a house in Covent Garden, Charles established the rather grandly named Museum Minervae. It would open its doors to pupils eager to learn 'foreign languages, mathematics, painting, architecture, riding, fortification, antiquities and the science of medals'. But of course, only to those who could 'prove themselves gentlemen'. Inigo Jones, that supreme genius of architecture, would not have qualified. More practical was the help the king gave to the Mortlake Manufactory, which produced superb tapestries and objects crafted in gold and silver.

Many of them found their way into the newly decorated royal quarters at Hampton Court – a palace so small that the king's servants had to camp in the grounds. Charles's enemies made much of his twenty-four 'palaces', many of which were merely hunting-boxes, or so dilapidated as to be virtually uninhabitable. Richmond, Eltham and Nonesuch all came into this latter category; Greenwich, except for the unfinished Queen's House, was still Elizabethan; Windsor, more of a fortress than a dwelling

5. Inigo Jones' design, never executed, for a new Whitehall

place, was at least more compact and convenient than rambling, antiquated Whitehall. At one point Inigo Jones, the Works Surveyor, drew up plans for a new Whitehall Palace (see plate 5), but to no avail. The king and his French queen had to be content with replacing the heavy Henrician furniture and laying rugs instead of rushes on the stone flags.

Meanwhile, much of Jones's architectural talent was being channelled into designing stage-sets for that favourite Stuart spectacle – the masque. These costumed pageants (see plate 6) –

6. Inigo Jones' costume designs for a court masque

a mixture of singing, dancing, poetry and fantastic stage effects – reached their zenith under James's queen, Anne of Denmark, forced to occupy herself while her husband occupied his time with Buckingham. The life of the neglected queen, according to her critics, was one of 'continued maskerado', with Anne herself playing all the principal parts, and wearing often a fortune of £100,000 in jewels. Charles's queen, Henrietta Maria, was more dignified but scarcely less extravagant. Small, dark and vivacious, she had Gallic tastes and a Gallic temper when crossed. Nevertheless, her self-effacing sympathy at the time of Buckingham's assassination had won her Charles's everlasting gratitude and devotion. Ever ready to depend on someone close to him, the king had turned to his wife for support. It was she who took Buckingham's place in his heart. In return, he pandered to every frivolous whim of hers: new clothes – she set a fashion for plain, creamy satins, her own favourite colours being amber and pale watery-green; her own retinue of the most dashing gentlemen at court to escort her to the theatre and thus scandalize her subjects; every conceivable diversion and amusement from dwarfs and blackamoors to a tribe of pet monkeys. A dwarf in full armour once jumped out of a pie in front of her, and stood solemnly at attention among the dishes on the table. And, like her predecessor, Queen Henrietta Maria loved the masque. Indeed, she loved it so much that she took the main part in *Chloridia*, confessing afterwards that it helped her with her English. It was not considered inappropriate for a monarch to turn actress. On the contrary, these masques, like Rubens's painting in the Banqueting Hall of James I among the gods and equal with them, reinforced the Stuart view of the divine nature of kingship. It was not for nothing that King James, who wrote a defence of absolutism entitled, *The Trew Law of Free Monarchies*, chose to appear enthroned in a masque as Pan, the universal god. Similarly, *The Masque of Queens* was written as homage to the royal consort. It was written by Ben Jonson, the poet and playwright, whose dramatic collaboration with Inigo Jones lasted for twenty-six years. It was this fruitful partnership which gave the masque its artistic worth. From Jonson's pen, the verse flowed, rich and sparkling; as a result of Jones's ingenious scenery designs, clouds moved, angels flew, devils sank inexorably into Hell, and fairy princes did, indeed, live in magical palaces. But when they quarrelled over precedence, the court took the Surveyor's side, despite his being, according to the papal agent, *huomo vanissimo* (a very vain man). Jonson abruptly lost the royal patronage and lived out his last six years poverty-stricken and alone. It could have given him no comfort to know that his rival flourished, the self-appointed arbiter of taste at court, frequently to be seen accompanying the king and queen round the royal picture collection, pointing out an authorship here, fixing a value there, his advice appreciated, and acted upon immediately.

Charles and Henrietta Maria were inseparable but by now even the rare sight of a happy royal couple counted for little in the face of the court's increasing isolation and unpopularity. The queen, that 'foreigner', was the focus of much of the discontent. The 'Queen's Party' began to be viewed with as much suspicion as Buckingham had been. Signs of kingly high-handedness were blamed on the French sense of royal autocracy; there was a genuine fear that a popish queen might wean Charles away from his duties to the English church. Such fears were irrational, but all the more dangerous for being rooted in prejudice. Nevertheless, characteristically, the king and queen chose to ignore them. Papal agents came and went at court. Mass was celebrated daily in Inigo Jones's richly classical Queen's Chapel, completed in 1627 at St James's Palace, and still in use there today. Most damaging of all, the powerful and, to some, sinister Jesuit Order made several well-publicized conversions. To the anti-papists, the king had as good as returned to Rome.

By itself this would not have been enough to condemn him, but Charles had earned the emnity of a powerful and vociferous cross-section of country gentry, those in the mainstream of English life who had never breathed the rarified air at court. James I had sown the seeds of their mistrust: now his son was to harvest them.

☙☙☙☙☙☙

COUNTRY LIFE

☙☙☙☙☙☙

NEITHER Charles I nor his courtiers can have given much thought to it, but of his 4 to 5 million subjects, an estimated four-fifths lived off the land. London, with its population of some 250,000 at the beginning of the seventeenth century, was the only community large enough for us to think of as a city. Bristol, Norwich and York were glorified villages of perhaps 10,000 people each. Manchester and Birmingham were hamlets, even by seventeenth-century standards. The rest of the populace lived in scattered and isolated villages, separated by mile upon mile of open heath, marshland and the remains of the old English forests. Communications were slow and news could take several weeks or more to reach the farthest-flung communities. Years later, when the century was well advanced, it still meant eleven hours hard riding for a traveller to cover twenty-five miles on the rutted roads. Small wonder that the fickle ways and transient fashions at court had little effect on the rural life of England, which had hardly changed since Elizabethan times and was to last, at any rate, until the upheaval of the Civil War.

THE COUNTRY GENTRY

We do not have a gentry today and when we use the word we probably give it the meaning that it had in Victorian times. The gentry then were a definite stratum of society, occupying a well-defined position in between the aristocracy and the middle classes. In seventeenth-century England there was no substantial middle

7. The English Gentleman: from an engraving dated 1630

class, only a few merchants aspiring to be landed. Englishmen were divided not as noble and commoner, but as 'gentle' and 'simple', and the term 'gentle' encompassed men from very different worlds. The high-minded Puritan squires, for example, many of whom like John Hampden opposed the king in Parliament, had as much right to be called 'gentry' as any royalist lord. They were landowners, certainly, and could boast of a coat-of-arms; they had the right to wear swords and demand satisfaction by duelling. Thus, the *Court and Times* of March 1627–8 noted:

> The House of Commons was both yesterday and today as full as one could sit by another. And they say it is the most noble, magnanimous assembly that ever these walls contained; and I heard a lord estimate they were able to buy the upper house (His Majesty only excepted) thrice over, notwithstanding there be of lords temporal to the number of 118. And what lord in England would be followed by so many freeholders as some of those are?

Thus, the Crown's attempts to raise money at the expense of the landowning gentry – by raising the fines on inheritance, increasing the rents on Crown lands, redrawing boundaries to benefit the Crown – met with the united opposition of a landowning and 'gentle' Parliament. 'I am surprised,' commented James I after a gruelling session, 'that my ancestors should have permitted such an institution to come into existence.' The gentry, naturally, had other views. 'Like columns do upprop the fabric of a building', reads the engraving, dated 1633, on the market-hall at Leominster, 'so noble gentry do support the honor of a kingdom'.

Inevitably, some of the hard-pressed gentry were ruined by the Stuart onslaught on their purses, yet as a class they were bound to survive. The strength of the gentry lay in its fluidity. Old landed families might decline and face eclipse; only sons mortgage their fortunes to the moneylenders or squander them at cards, but there were always others to take their place. New gentry who had grown rich on the profits from cheap monastic lands; merchants eager to acquire respectability along with an estate – these were the replacements for those who, as Richard Whalley, a gentleman of Sussex wrote, had 'consumed their whole estates, even to one

8. George Herbert, poet and parish priest

foot of ground, [some] with much ado to get winding sheets; some died under hedges'.

What were these country gentry like? When we think of them, we tend to think of Fielding's picture in *Tom Jones* of an eighteenth-century red-cheeked, rustic country squire, muttering over his beer about popishness and fancy, foreign ways. And many of the early seventeenth-century gentry cannot have been all that different. George Herbert (see plate 8), the Anglican poet and divine, compared them to their own sheep: 'Most are gone to grass and in the pasture lost.' It seems true to say that they were, on the whole, a rough and ready lot. It was only a small circle of London-based sophisticates who knew enough to patronize Donne and Shakespeare, Hobbes and Jonson. History, the Bible and theology were all that the average respectable gentleman read – if he read much of anything. Similarly with architecture: the gentry lived, many of them, in the manors of their forbears, still recognizable a hundred years later as the semi-fortified strongholds built to withstand siege during the Wars of the Roses. Inside they were as cramped and dark as any of the yeomen's houses which are our 'country cottages' of today. Yet despite the changing fashions in London, the gentry were in no great hurry to replace them. Indeed, the vogue for classical country houses did not become widespread until later in the century. Meanwhile, there was something lucky, if not prophetic, about the country gentry's dogged unfashionableness. Small windows and sturdy walls made their houses easy to defend in another civil war, yet to come.

This is a description of the home of one typical seventeenth-century country gentleman, Henry Hastings of Dorset. He lived in:

> A house not so neatly kept as to shame him or his dirty shoes, the great hall strewed with marrow bones, full of hawks' perches, hounds, spaniels and terriers; the upper sides of the hall hung with the fox-skins of this and last year's skinning, here and there a polecat intermixed, guns and keepers' and huntsmens' poles in abundance. The parlor . . . as properly furnished; on a great hearth paved with brick lay some terriers and the choicest hounds and spaniels; seldom but two of the great chairs and litters of young cats in them . . . he having always three or four attending him at dinner, and a little white round stick of fourteen inches long lying by his trencher, that he might defend such meat as he had no mind to part with to them.

The main impression is not so much one of squalor as of chaos – inevitable when one room was used for so many different functions. The early Stuarts followed the Elizabethan custom of the Great Hall as the centre of the home. The family ate there, entertained there, transacted their business and did their day-to-day living there, under the full public gaze of countless servants and dependants. Just how many dependants there could be in a rich or noble household is illustrated by the unfortunate experience of Lord Berkeley. So plagued was he by constant demands on his hospitality that whenever the unwelcome guests – 'captains, scholars, poets, past courtiers, and the like' – looked like staying too long, his only recourse was to close down his castle. With his wife, children and a few servants, he would then move to a small manor – and wait for the hordes to move on.

Strictly speaking, Lord Berkeley was at fault. To keep open house was the duty of any gentleman. His other functions were to provide work, alleviate need and generally aid the smooth running of the Poor Law. Some gentry also had to administer the Law if they were Justices of the Peace. If they objected to their role as hosts, it was because of what it cost them and not, as we might imagine, because of any lack of privacy. Privacy was essentially an eighteenth-century concept. Not until towards the end of the century were separate dining-rooms introduced, so that the family could eat unscrutinized. In the meantime, smaller houses would have a parlour, as an alternative to the hurly-burly of the Hall. The larger mansions could boast two or three such panelled chambers. Indeed, they were sometimes given names to distinguish them from each other. The Blue Chamber, the White Chamber, the Great Parlour, the Winter Parlour – such descriptions appear regularly in seventeenth-century household records. References to colour are particularly frequent, reflecting a deeply felt hunger for light in the dark, poorly lit interiors. To us some of the colour schemes would seem garish: the Earl of Buccleuch's bed, for example, upholstered in red trimmed with green lace. Later on, the Duke of Lauderdale, Charles II's dandified minister would travel with a monstrous four-poster, curtained in purple damask. Attempts to brighten the walls at the beginning of the century resulted in elaborate murals of flowers, fruit and heraldic motifs. By the mid-century, this was considered barbaric. The taste now was for restrained panelling, hung with tapestries or gilt-tooled leather. Such were the dictates of fashion that, when wood was not available, the panelling was painted on, in a suitable 'walnut tree' colour – rather like the plastic disguised as wood that is in use today. The floors were also of wood, polished but uncarpeted, for carpets like dining-rooms were an eighteenth-century innovation. Seventeenth-century gentle families would have kept carpets, if they had them, on a table, not on the floor.

However, where there were stone flags, the general tendency was to cover them with rush mats sewn together by a tailor.

Jacobean furniture was simple. The bed was the most important article, heavily curtained in silk or velvet for warmth (see colour plate 5). The master of the house, attired in night-cravat, night-shirt, bedsocks and a satin night-cap, would climb in and shut the curtains tight. His servants would already have heated the feather mattress with a warming-pan, and arranged the linen sheets, woollen blankets and embroidered quilts. If he was lucky a fire would burn in the grate throughout the winter, for his house was often cold enough for water to freeze as soon as it was poured. Apart from the bed, his room would hold a ewer and basin stand, close-stool and chamber-pot. Bathrooms were an unheard-of luxury and even soap was scarce. 'Love you to be cleane,' pleaded Sir John Harington in 1608 in *The Englishman's Doctor*, 'for from . . . our cradles let us abhor uncleanness, which neither nature nor reason can endure.' But the English gentry could endure it. Sir John's advice went unheeded as did his peculiar invention, the water-closet. Lice and fleas infested even the richest houses and chamber-pots emptied out of windows made the town streets open sewers. Public baths had at least made life more bearable in earlier centuries, but from 1600 onwards, little thought was given to hygiene. Instead, housewives scattered herbs. A seventeenth-century doctor recommended 'a handsome room, well-matted or hung with tapestries all around and paved below with rosemary, pennyroyal, oregano, marjoram, lavender, sage and other similar herbs'.

If the bedchamber was utilitarian, the other rooms were scarcely more comfortable. Seating in many early Stuart households was still at the bench and trestle stage. An exceptionally splendid mansion might have boasted some chairs which were upholstered, either with horse-hair padding, or rush or cane seats. If it was large enough it might also have contained a picture gallery, a feature of many Elizabethan houses, which remained popular under the Stuarts. Not that many of the Stuart gentry were knowledgeable about art: the only pictures they liked were those inherited from their ancestors, serried ranks of Elizabethans,

9. The diarist, John Evelyn

wan-faced in their ruffs, painted on a gloomy background of
black-painted boards. A gentleman travelling in Holland was
aghast to find that, 'Every man's house is full of pictures, a vanity
that draweth on a charge.' Cultivated Englishmen who made the
pilgrimage to Italy wrote with fervour about the antiquities and
reported glowingly on the churches – but hardly mentioned art.
Only when confronted with the full splendour of the Sistine
chapel, did one of them make a grudging reference to 'that excell-
ent artificial painter called Michael Angelo Buonaretto'. Raphael

1. James I

2. George Villiers,
Duke of Buckingham

3. Rubens' ceiling
in the Banqueting
House, Whitehall

might never have lived for all the attention paid to him. An exception to this philistinism was the diarist John Evelyn (see plate 9), who travelled extensively and appreciatively in Italy during the years of the Civil War. So, too, was Thomas Howard, Earl of Arundel, who made his pilgrimage accompanied by Inigo Jones.

But most of the Stuart gentry preferred less aesthetic pastimes, like hunting, for example. This excerpt from the diary of the admittedly dull-witted Nicholas Assheton shows how a country squire in 1617 might have spent the summer months:

> MAY 2. Hunting the otter: killed one: taken another, quick, at Salley. Spent VId.
>
> MAY 12. Father Greenacres, mother, aunt Besse, John, wyffe, self, at ale. Sp. IVd.
>
> JUNE 11. Tryed for a fox, found none; rayne; wet thorough. Home agayne.
>
> JUNE 15. Sunday Trin. Parson preached; to Church. Aft. sermon; sp. VId. Home. To Church pson. preached.
>
> JUNE 16. Fox-hunting.
>
> JUNE 17. I and brother Greenacres to Portfield (rayne), then to Whalley; fox-hunting. To the pond: a duck and a dogg. To the Abbey: drunk there. Home . . .
>
> JUNE 24. Tryed for ye fox; found nothing. Towler lay at a rabbit, and wee stayed and wrought and took her.

For many, day after day, year after year, passed in a round of hare-coursing, fox-hunting, otter-spearing, badger-trapping and other such bloodthirsty pursuits (see plates 10 and 11), washed down by a nightly stint in the ale-house. 'Lord! What is man and sober?' wrote Richard Lovelace, who, as well as being a Cavalier poet, was a typical Kentish squire. Often the squire's companions were the local yeomen and tenant farmers if he lived too far away from his nearest gently-born neighbours. Small wonder, then, that he lacked finesse.

But what of the squire's lady who might have been expected to tame him? She was usually far too busy with her own tasks, as the

10 and 11. Seventeenth-century needlework: hunting scenes

seventeenth-century books on housewifery make clear. Gervase Markham, in writing *The English Huswife*, laid down some exacting standards. A 'huswife' must be:

> of chaste thought, stout courage, patient, untired, watchful, diligent, witty, pleasant, constant in friendship, full of good neighbourhood, wise in discourse . . . secret in her affairs, comfortable in her counsels, and generally skilful in all the worthy knowledges which do belong to her vocation.

What it added up to was grinding hard work for all except for the very rich. The seventeenth-century squire's lady was no Jane Austen heroine idling away the hours in the drawing-room. Her natural habitat was far more likely to be the kitchen – and the kitchen garden.

Each seventeenth-century country house was a self-supporting entity. It had to be when the long winters made the roads impassable. Food came from the estate; beer was brewed on the premises; fat was set aside to make soap and candles, and poultry feathers used to stuff pillows and mattresses. Intense preparation was the only guarantee of a comfortable winter with enough preserved fruit, pickled vegetables and salted beef for all to eat. Responsibility for all these tasks rested ultimately with the lady of the household. In lesser houses she was also expected to do the cooking.

The meals were formidable: meat, bread and ale for a six o'clock breakfast; every variety of meat and game from larks to venison for the main midday meal. The conscientious housewife provided a rich accompaniment of sauces as well as soups, salads and numerous custards and jellies. Between five o'clock and eight, the whole gastronomic extravaganza was repeated when a marginally less elaborate supper was served.

The other province of the housewife was the kitchen garden, source of her lore as a herbalist and healer. Herbal prescriptions, handed down through the generations, served the household well when no doctor was available. In 1629 John Parkinson, James I's apothecary, wrote a gardening book which became a bible for many households. His instructions on how to grow, among other plants, spinach, cucumber, melon and asparagus, show the rich variety of food cultivable even then. Certainly no seventeenth-century gardener ever thought of landscaping his garden: space was too valuable. Such frivolity he left to the eighteenth century and men like 'Capability' Brown, born in 1715.

Few seventeenth-century wives had ample time for leisure. Fewer still were sufficiently educated to make the most of what little time they had. The daughters of intellectual or Puritan families (who were taught to read in order to read the Bible) could count themselves fortunate indeed, if they had received a grounding in classics or theology. Their true destiny lay elsewhere. From the age of twelve onwards they could expect to leave their families and make the suitable marriage their parents had arranged for them. Such matches were carefully negotiated: minute attention was given to property and rank. The Stuart English were proud of their family trees and paid to have them lavishly bound and illustrated, but nevertheless a merchant's daughter might still marry a gentleman if she brought with her a large enough dowry. However, woe betide the daughter whose dowry chest was empty or whose husband appropriated her money and then neglected her. Shame also on those romantics who expected to marry for love. Such 'selfishness', as Lord Cork angrily informed his wayward son, would 'dash all my designs which concern myself and my house'.

In many cases, betrothal took place long before the marriage ceremony, to safeguard the interests of the parents and their children. There is a record of one such 'young wedding', presided over by the Bishop of Durham, in which the bride and groom were six and eight. 'They carry themselves very gravely, and love dearly', was the comment of a fond, if deluded, onlooker. In such circumstances the children returned to live with their parents until they reached a more marriageable age. But girls, still in their early teens, who took on the responsibility of a household, would find all too soon that they had grown old before their time. Even in the more leisured eighteenth century Jane Austen described a twenty-seven-year-old woman as 'middle-aged'.

THE CLERGY

A seventeenth-century parish priest was a more respected member of society than his lowly pre-Reformation predecessor, but he still had a long way to go before he could mingle freely with the gentry on more or less equal terms as an eighteenth-century parson could. Younger sons of the gentry in the seventeenth century did on occasion go into the church, but only into its upper echelons to become deans or bishops. Many of the ordinary parsons were lamentably poor and underprivileged, on a par with a yeoman rather than a squire. Archbishop Whitgift, Archbishop of Canterbury on James I's accession, calculated that of 9000 benefices, only 600 yielded sufficient income to support an educated man. Approximately half the vicars in England earned under £10 a year. As a result the candidates for priesthood were, many of them, ignorant men from lowly backgrounds. Most had no degree of any sort and less than half were licensed to preach. In any case, they seldom preached: some, like the idle Rector of Normanton 'because he was playing at the tables with the schoolmaster of Hambleton'; more often, they were too busy eking out a meagre living as subsistence farmers. Several even put their cattle out to graze in the churchyard. With few exceptions, a smattering of Latin was the full extent of their education. Nicholas Breton was appalled to greet a clergyman in Latin and receive the reply: 'My friend, I understand not your Greek.'

In theory, the parish priests were expected to derive income from the 'glebe' lands attached to the parsonage, as well as the tithes or tenths levied on the animals and produce of their parishioners. In practice, parishioners were naturally loath to part with the hard-earned fruit of their labours and there were few ways in which a clergyman could press them. Often, even the right to tithe was no longer his: many such rights had fallen to the Crown during Henry VIII's dissolution of the monasteries and were later re-distributed or sold to laymen. They, in turn, paid the clergy a pittance in compensation. For a clergyman to survive economically, his only hope was to become chaplain to a rich family, or, if he had the right connections, to hold more than one benefice at once. This 'pluralism' was an accepted practice. In the previous reign one bishop, the Bishop of St Asaph's, had held no less than sixteen livings.

The right to appoint to livings belonged usually to the local squire, if he had not sold his powers of patronage to another, third party. As a result the country clergy were dominated by the gentry in their area. And chosen as they were for their pliability, they were not likely to protest, whatever the circumstances. There is a record of an Essex gentleman striking his curate in church and telling him: 'Thou art a dunce and a bold dunce. I will make thee neither parson nor vicar. But I will not call thee knave.' We do not know what the curate had done but even if he had done nothing, he had no means of defending himself. Financially, he was totally at the mercy of his squire. Some clergy even found it wise to reflect their masters' religious preferences, be they High church or Low.

> Our Doctor differs not much from the weathercock in the steeple, sometimes he is all for ceremony, sometimes indifferent, sometimes against –

so ran one cynical parish's verdict on its vicar.

Not all the clergy were so unworthy. The church sheltered many scholars and saints even among its parish priests. George Herbert, the priestly poet was one such exceptional man who believed that

> A verse may find him who a sermon flies,
> And turn delight into a sacrifice.

'My poor abilities in Poetry,' he wrote to his mother at the age of sixteen, 'shall be all, and ever consecrated to God's glory.' Yet before he took holy orders in 1630, Herbert had seemed bound for high state office. He came from an eminent family and was well known in court circles as a poet, intellect and wit. Worldly and ambitious, he made his first mark as Public Orator of Cambridge where, as his friend and later biographer, Izaak Walton remarked, 'his clothes seemed to prove that he put too great a value on his parts and parentage'. It was a surprise to many of his contemporaries when Herbert discovered a religious vocation in his thirties, but they were shocked and aghast when he decided to spend his life as a lowly parish priest. 'Losing himself in an humble way' was not considered suitable employment for a gentleman, who had less uncomfortable options open to him, even within the church. One acquaintance, according to Walton, accused him of 'disparag'ing himself by so dirty an employment'. Herbert's reply is given in Walton's *Life*:

> That the thought of what he had done, would prove Musick to him at Midnight; and that the omission of it would have upbraided and made discord in his Conscience, whensoever he should pass by that place ... let me tell you, I would not willingly pass one day of my life without comforting a sad soul, or shewing mercy; and I praise God for this occasion.

Ironically, it was Herbert's very worldliness that gave his devotional poetry such impact. Deep emotions are expressed in a courtly urbane style. He draws on ordinary experience and everyday affairs to illustrate the inner struggles of a man of God, and this realism gives a sharp edge to his poetry, saving it from woolly emotionalism. Listen to him, for example, undergoing a crisis in his faith:

> My mirth and edge was lost; a blunted knife
>   Was of more use than I.
> Thus thinne and lean without a fence or friend,
> I was blown through with ev'ry storm and winde.

In the same vein, although he was not a clergyman and indeed was not converted until 1648, Henry Vaughan also wrote religious poetry. His poems are more mysterious and less empirical than Herbert's. His images are drawn from nature: the sun, the wind, the sky, the stars. The 'deep but dazzling darkness of God' is one of his most memorable phrases, and another: 'Bright shootes of everlastingness.'

Richard Crashaw was the poet of the High church and Laudian ritual. In 1643 he left England, living first in France and then in Rome, where he became a Catholic. Like the Catholic mystics he wrote of the ecstasy of adoration, using sensuous and even erotic metaphors to convey his love of God.

It was a whole world away from the rarified circle of religious poets to the country parsonage standing alongside the village church. Here, the average clergyman lived a life fairly similar to that of a prosperous yeoman. He would own some oak tables and settles and, if he was lucky, a little silver. More important to him would be his animals and the tools with which to work his land. If he was able to afford it, he would hire some labourers to help him and his wife would employ a servant girl in the kitchen. She herself might well be the daughter of a yeoman; she would attend the women in childbirth and occasionally visit the sick. Sometimes her husband would be consulted over land disputes between farmers; sometimes, if he knew a little law, he would help the local JP.

As late as 1670, Eachard, Master of St Catherine's College, Cambridge, was complaining about *Contempt of the Clergy*. Nevertheless, a forceful vicar could make his voice heard locally. Ben Jonson, in *The Magnetick Lady*, mentions such a man:

> He is the prelate of the parish here;
> And governs all the dames; appoints the cheer;
> Writes down the bills of fare; pricks all the guests;
> Makes all the matches and the marriage feasts
>   . . . draws all the parish wills . . .
> Comforts the widow, and the fatherless,
> In funeral sack.

Some of the clergy were even beginning to make their influence felt nationally. In 1603 James I, riding south, had confronted a deputation of Puritan churchmen. They had presented him with the Millenary Petition – so called because 1000 clergy were supposed to have signed it – demanding reform of abuses in the Church of England. Among their targets were uneducated parsons, absentee vicars and pluralists. In return, in 1604, King James called the Hampton Court Conference, which, although it was ultimately responsible for producing the Authorized Version of the Bible, had also the less beneficial effect of bringing out into the open the rift between the Puritans and the ecclesiastical hierarchy. In the following reign, the animosity became even more intense, heightened by Puritan suspicions of a return to Rome at the instigation of the king. Then in 1633 Charles I appointed as Archbishop of Canterbury, William Laud, vigorous, reforming, but an avowed enemy of Puritanism (see plate 12). 'Laudism' was instantly unpopular and not only with the Puritans. The country gentry saw it as a challenge to their hitherto invincible position in the parishes. Laudian doctrine proposed the exaltation of clergy over laity, insisting that the clergy were responsible only to God. Newly confident, some vicars flexed their spiritual muscles by standing out against their squires. Laud's own high-handedness did much to inflame the gentry's growing anti-clericalism. When the head of the legal profession, Lord Chief Justice Richardson, was accused of leniency to the Puritans on his circuit, Laud insulted him publicly before the Council. His Lordship was forbidden to ride the western circuit. 'I have been almost choked,' he raged, 'by a pair of lawn sleeves.'

To the House of Commons, all of whom were gentry and many of whom were Puritans, it looked like a conspiracy between

12. Puritan cartoon, satirizing Laud and the court bishops. The most godly of the three clergymen is on the left, holding a bible in his hand and untouched by the worldly ambition of the others

church and king. Inevitably, fearing a return to the absolutism of Henry VIII's Cardinal Wolsey, or even the sinister example of Cardinal Richelieu in France, their sympathies were with the Puritans. What had begun as a struggle within the church spread to encompass Parliament, and the king.

THE YEOMEN AND FARM LABOURERS

The King of Naples, said Shakespeare, is not so rich as an English yeoman. Comparatively speaking, it was not such an exaggeration. The English yeoman was self-sufficient; he had no wants that he could not satisfy. He could live off his land (see plate 13), build his house – of stone, brick or oak beams and plaster, according to the natural resources in his area – make his

13. Ploughing

14. Country scene. From a contemporary illustration

furniture and construct his own farm implements. His wife could spin (see plate 14), weave, sew his clothes, help with the harvesting, and set his table with good 'yeoman's fare . . . bread, beer and beef . . . no kickshaws [fancy food], full dishes, whole bellyfuls'. She could also sell his surplus produce in the market.

But, more important, he was answerable to no one. His status as a yeoman derived from his being able to count on forty shillings a year income from his own freehold land. This was also his qualification for voting in the county elections, a privilege he exercised, often with surprising independence.

Within the yeoman class, there were vast differences of wealth and status. At one end of the scale, a small yeoman might be no more than a subsistence farmer. Yet others owned vast acreages. Some of them like Adam Eyre of Yorkshire deserved to be called gentlemen. Adam Eyre was eventually afforded this distinction but only on his tombstone. Although a yeoman was strictly speaking, a freeholder, there were many who, though they lived as yeomen, held their lands by tenure. Often the tenure had passed from father to son for generations, so that the family felt they had a 'propertied' right to it.

As they differed, so too did their houses, but most yeomen at least lived quite comfortably. A yeoman's house might have one or two storeys: it was almost certain to have a milkhouse and other out-buildings adjoining it. Inside there would be a living-room with an open fire on which to cook, and a deep recess for kitchen utensils. The beds would be placed wherever there was room, among the oak tables, chests, settles, and a few sturdy chairs.

In his fields the yeoman toiled unceasingly. The land was an exacting master and each season had its tasks. A page from Adam Eyre's journal gives us a valuable example of the work he set himself in a single day. His first duty was to oversee his labourers and set one to work harrowing, another building a wall, a third making general repairs around the farm. Only then was he himself free to visit a neighbour and buy a cheese before returning home to start work on a new pigsty. Even when this was finished his day was not over. With his workmen he hewed and chopped wood till evening.

Despite their hard lives, many yeomen had other jobs besides farming. In East Anglia and Wiltshire they spun and wove for the flourishing cloth industry. Others did odd jobs as tanners, carpenters or blacksmiths. There are even records of yeomen who kept ale-houses. To sell their goods well, they had to attend the weekly markets and pit their wits against the sharp-eyed merchants. There are several instances of yeomen proving astute businessmen, knowing how, for example, to hoard their wheat to gain the benefit of a price-rise. Richard Brome's play, *The Sparagus Garden*, asserts that 'knavery' was as common in 'russet wool' as in 'proudest purple'.

The yeoman's wife also went to market to sell the produce of her dairy and kitchen garden. If contemporaries like the chronicler Thomas Fuller are to be believed, there was nearly always a surplus. The farmer, he wrote in 1642, 'shall have as many joints as dishes; no straggling joint of a sheep in the midst of a pasture of grasse, beset with sallads on every side, but solid, substantial food'. The food, if always 'solid and substantial', varied according to the season and the area. There was fresh beef or mutton only from midsummer until Christmas. In the winter the farmer's wife made do with game or salted beef, or fish, when meat was prohibited, during Lent. At all other times of the year meat was so plentiful, that foreigners were amazed to see the English discard the feet and entrails of the beasts they killed. Extra nourishment was to be had from 'frumenty', a dish of wheat boiled in milk and seasoned with sugar and cinnamon. The 'small beer' brewed at home or by country innkeepers was high in calories and rich in calcium, vitamins and sugar. In the next century when the English became a nation of tea instead of beer-drinkers, the effect on their health was noticeably detrimental.

'To thrive, a yeoman must wive,' wrote Thomas Tusser, the rhymer. The reverse was not so true. A wry little epitaph to the wife of a Gloucestershire yeoman is a testament to the hard life and arduous duties of a seventeenth-century farmer's wife:

> From my sad cradle to my sable chest,
> Poor pilgrim, I did find few months of rest.

Of course, while they were at home, the yeoman's wife was helped by her unmarried daughters. But all too soon they left to set up households of their own, and the need to provide suitable dowries would be an additional charge upon their hard-pressed fathers. The daughters of yeomen married mostly into the yeomanry, but they could also find husbands outside its ranks – amongst the schoolmasters and clergymen of the district. These were also the professions open to the yeoman's younger sons. A clever and ambitious boy might go on from grammar school to university, but even a university education would not make much difference to his prospects. The eldest son, no matter how much education he had received as a matter of course followed his father on to the land.

By the mid-seventeenth century many yeomen and even yeomen's wives could read and write, but to some this may have seemed an unfruitful accomplishment. 'We can learn to plough and harrow, sow and reap, and prune, thresh and fan, winnow and grind, brew and bake', the writer Nicholas Breton made his yeoman boast 'and all without a book'. There is some truth and much experience behind the saying. As the century advanced and Puritan sympathies grew, religion became the main intellectual outlet of many country people able to read and write. William Honiwell records a dinner with his Devon neighbours in which the talk was all 'arguments of Scripture'. Adam Eyre, not a deeply religious man, nevertheless read mainly theological writings, simply because they were available. In the mid-seventeenth century talk of religion was in the air: for many it became their staple intellectual diet. 'This day I rested at home, and spent most of the day reading,' records Adam Eyre. He also built bookshelves and lent books to his neighbours. If he and others like him were typical, then as a class, the yeomen were well equipped to choose sides in the Civil War.

The farm labourers had no such problems of choice. There was little political or religious consciousness among the peasantry. In medieval times they had risen in revolt but in Stuart England even during the unsettled years following the Civil War when 30,000 political pamphlets were published questioning every aspect of the status quo, the peasantry did not respond. On the contrary, quite another picture of them is given in a letter from the gently born Dorothy Osborne. 'You ask me how I pass my time here,' she writes from the country to her lover. And then:

> The heat of the day is spent in reading or working, and about six or seven o'clock I walk out into a common that lies hard by the house where a great many wenches keep sheep and cows and sit in the shade singing of ballads. I talk to them and find they want nothing to make them the happiest people in the world, but the knowledge that they are so. Most commonly when we are in the midst of our discourse, one looks about her and spies her cows going into the corn, and then away they all run as if they had wings at their heels.

An idyllic picture, though probably not over-accurate. We know, for example, that many labourers lived in primitive turf, mud or clay-lump dwellings, so poorly furnished that they slept with logs for pillows instead of bolsters. Music they did have, in the shape of wandering minstrels. The Duke of Stettin, visiting England in 1603, was charmed by the 'beautiful music of violas and pandoras, for in all England it is the custom that even in small villages the musicians wait on you for a small fee. In the morning about wakening time they stand outside the chamber playing religious hymns'. An English traveller's observations abroad are more to the point. He was shocked, on his journeys in Europe, to see the state of the foreign peasantry, with their 'wooden shoes and straw hats' and only 'grass herbs and roots' to eat.

For, in spite of everything, the English labourers were not badly provided for. They were freemen by law (unlike their French and German contemporaries) and though underpaid, they had plenty to eat. Until he married, the agricultural labourer generally lived in his employer's farmhouse and shared bed and board with his family. Even afterwards, the ties remained close. Many labourers had served the same family for generations. This, then, was the reason for their conservatism.

꧁꧁꧁꧁꧁

TOWN LIFE

꧁꧁꧁꧁꧁

To talk of towns in seventeenth-century England is rather mis-
leading: what they called towns, we would certainly call villages.
Thomas Wilson in 1600, writing on 'the State of England',
described as 'great towns' communities with sometimes only 1000
people. The reason for this is clear: there was no factory system
and little organized industry. The workers in the cloth trade,
England's biggest export, worked at home in family units and
sold their work to middlemen. The spinners and weavers who
sent kerseys to York and worsteds to Norwich were often small-
holders with a few acres, or yeoman farmers working part-time.
Even in the country market towns, some of which had up to 5000
inhabitants, farms and orchards lined the main street alongside
houses and shops. The average townsman still kept some sort of
link with agriculture, probably a smallholding which he farmed
on the outskirts of the town. From the towns the countryside was
not only easily accessible: it encroached right on to the old stone
boundary walls (see plate 15) and surrounded the new 'suburbs'
of houses beyond. There was scarcely a market cross in England
more than a mile away from open fields. In *Paradise Lost* John
Milton writes of town-dwellers

> Long in populous city pent
> Where houses thick and sewers annoy the air,
> Forth issuing on a summer's morn to breathe
> Among the pleasant villages and farms
> Adjoined.

4. Henrietta Maria
by Van Dyck

5. The Lapierre Canopy,
Hardwick Hall

6.
Charles I
dining in
state at
Whitehall

Matth: 23, Marc: 12, Prou: 27, 2 Cor: 10. 90
O mnia vero opera sua faciunt, vt videantur ab ho‑
minibus, etc. Laudet te alterius, et non labia sua, etc,
Qui autem gloriatur, in domino glorietur, Non, etc

Trita lacerna nimis sua sit licet, attamen asses
Ut propter paucos iste superbit inops,
Sic multi factis tarde insidiantur honestis,
Quos tamen haud sese concelebrare pudet,

15. Seventeenth-century walled town

Yet the town population was on the increase. By the end of the seventeenth century it had grown substantially. This can be attributed directly to the expansion of two industries, coal – a result of the current 'lament of deforestation' – and shipbuilding, for ships were needed to carry the coal. The advent of the Industrial Revolution was clearly signposted, even though it was still a long way off. In the meantime there was only one place in the seventeenth century where true city life could be experienced, and that place was London.

LONDON

In Elizabethan times the 'Queene of Cities' occupied a relatively small area in the midst of green fields, where the citizens could ride, stroll or hunt duck. Jonson mentions the sandy wastes of 'Chelsey' and 'All the grasse that Rumney yeelds'. Dotted around

the city were small outlying villages with country inns which the
citizens could visit on their days off, very much as we do on our
weekends nowadays. We know that Islington had a famous tavern
where 'Londoners flocked to taste its White Pot – a kind of
custard.

Nevertheless, by the beginning of the seventeenth century,
London was spreading (see plate 16), especially westwards towards
Whitehall to meet the demand for houses from the courtiers and
ambitious gentry – 'those swarms of gentry,' grumbled James I,
'who through the instigation of their wives . . . did neglect their
country hospitality and cumber the city'. Nothing remains today
of the great white palace itself, save Inigo Jones's classical
Banqueting House (see plate 17), sole survivor of a disastrous fire
in 1698. But at the beginning of the seventeenth century, the area
around Whitehall and Westminster – only a mile or two from the
city itself – was a thriving community. In the Strand, overlooking
the river, the nobles built their palaces. To serve their needs, a
group of enterprising tradesmen opened an Exchange of luxury
shops nearby in 1609. Already the area – seat of Parliament and

16. Visscher's map of London, 1616

17. Banqueting House, Whitehall, built 1619–22

the principal law courts – was acquiring most of the parapher-
nalia of a London season – parks, and pleasure gardens, theatres
and a transport system to ferry the gentry to their various engage-
ments. The ordinary citizens disliked the growing coach trade
which added to the congestion of the narrow, cobbled streets.
'They keep a vile swaggering in coaches nowadays,' wrote
Thomas Dekker and Thomas Middleton in *The Roaring Girl* in
1611, 'the highways are stopped with them.' They were also a
drain on the citizens' pockets, for with no highways authority,
each householder was responsible for repairing the road outside
his house. The watermen, too, resented this incursion into their
traditional market. In *An Arrant Thief*, (1632), John Taylor
voiced their fears of competition:

> All sorts of men work all the means they can
> To make a 'Thief' of every waterman,
> And as it were in one consent they join
> To trot by land i' the dirt and save their coin.
> Against the ground, we stand and knock our heels,
> Whilst all our profit runs away on wheels.

But coaches were necessary if a gentleman was to get from place to place quickly enough to enjoy all the delights that London could offer in a single day. The diary of Sir Humphrey Mildmay, an Essex landowner, reveals a never-ending round of spectacle and pleasure. Sir Humphrey went a-maying in Hyde Park, swimming and boating on the Thames, played at cards and dice with his friends and attended the theatre sometimes twice a week. We know that he saw *Othello* in 1635. When he had nothing else to do he went to watch the king dining in state (see Houckgeest's painting colour plate 6) or to some such city activity as the Lord Mayor's show.

There was no love between court and city. The poorest courtiers (see plate 18) looked down on the richest city merchants (see plate 19), considering them dull, parsimonious and avaricious and sneered at their over-dressed wives. Even when the exceptionally able Lionel Cranfield was given high office by James I, there were those at court who wondered how a simple merchant could participate in affairs of state. Ben Jonson reflected this feeling when he made a character say of a merchant in *Cynthia's Revels*: 'Tis thus, a dull plodding face, still looking in a direct line, forward: there is no great matter in this face.'

18. Seventeenth-century courtier and his lady

19. Seventeenth-century merchant and his wife

Of course, many of the merchant class were merely small shop-keepers or struggling brokers in wool and grain. But some of the East India Company grandees, the aldermen and heads of livery companies, lived in splendid style within the city confines in mansions with gardens and even stables. That the court would not accept them however rich they were, must have irked them considerably. Wits like Nicolas Breton mocked their lack of lineage and the fact that the 'son of What-lack-ye was become the only right-worshipful'. In view of this, it was inevitable that the city would take the Puritan side in the Civil War. In 1643 the tradesmen turned out in force to defend the gates of the City of London when it looked as if Charles I's army would march on them. Do not marry a courtier, the merchant urged his daughter in Thomas Dekker's *Shoemaker's Holiday*, for they were 'silken fellows, painted images'. 'No, my fine mouse, marry me with a gentleman grocer like my Lord Mayor, your father, a grocer is a sweet trade; plums, plums.'

With their Puritan sympathies, the merchants were sober, respectable and religious men. Their talk, apart from business, was often of the latest sermons. Long evenings were spent discussing difficult Bible passages or reading aloud simplistic religious fables. Stories about a woman being saved from fire by prayer, or a Sabbath-breaker, struck by lightning were dismissed by Jonson in *The Malcontents* as 'Lozenges of Sanctified Sincerity'. Some merchants knew better how to enjoy themselves: they frequented the taverns which, according to Sir Thomas Middleton numbered more than 1000 in 1613; and, like the rest of London, they went to the theatre. The rich Londoner in Jonson's *Poetaster*, uneasily entertaining courtiers at his splendid town house, says loftily, 'At your ladyship's service,' and then adds in a confidential aside, 'I got that speech by seeing a play last day, and it did me some grace now.'

In Stuart London the playhouses (see plate 20) were on the south side of the river, on the Southwark bank of the Thames alongside the Bear Garden or circus. Idle students from the Inns of Court and fashionable young gallants would be rowed across by watermen from Westminster or the Temple. Performances were given each afternoon and night and were universally popular, although at night the burning pitch which lighted the wooden theatres made fire a real hazard. Thomas Coriat, the writer, considered 'our stately playhouses in England' unrivalled 'for apparal shows of music'. Certainly, the whole of London went to them. The actors and authors had two distinct audiences. On the stage itself or in the stalls sat their patrons, the fine gentlemen, who helped to maintain the theatres by their gifts. In the standing area the unwashed mass of pimply apprentices and sweaty artisans jostled and craned and offered their pennies to the collectors with their locked collection-boxes. A fanfare heralded each performance but did not quieten the audience, who continued to eat and drink and smoke and shout their appreciation or abuse. Generally, they were appreciative even when the play was an old one, re-worked and given a new, topical slant. Even Shakespeare was adept at this, while in 1632 Donald Lupton said of the playwrights:

> They are as crafty with an old play as bawds with old faces. The one puts on a new fresh colour, and the other a new face and name.

20. Playhouses on the south side of the River Thames

The more sober Puritans disapproved of such levity but it was
1642 before they succeeded in closing the theatres, and the re-
opening of them in 1660 shows that the closure was against the
general will. Meanwhile, every gallant and fop, according to
Return From Parnassus, misquoted *Romeo and Juliet* to his mistress, secreted *Venus and Adonis* under his pillow and displayed
'sweet Mr Shakespeare's' picture prominently in his study at the
court (see plate 21).

21. William Shakespeare

'Sweet Mr Shakespeare' and his like, other literary men such as
John Donne and Jonson, provided a link between court and city.
Great actors like Richard Burbage were known to both merchants
and courtiers; playwrights like Ben Jonson had a whole range of
social contacts from tavern-keepers to that great patroness, Lucy,
Countess of Bedford. 'Rare poems aske rare friends,' wrote
Jonson, sending Donne's work to Lady Bedford, and indeed, he
did consider John Donne 'the first poet in the world in some
things'. Jonson himself had so many poetic imitators and followers that they were known humourously as 'the tribe of Ben'.

London was a magnet for seventeenth-century writers, the only place, as the historian Clarendon put it, where they could find 'study and conversation'. Some, of course, had been born there like John Milton, son of a scrivener, or Robert Herrick, the poet, who complained about his 'banishment' to a Devon vicarage. John Donne, who came from a rich city ironmongering family, gives us plenty of glimpses of seventeenth-century London in his poetry. For example, the streets where

> . . . sly beggars narrowly
> Watch motions of the giver's hand and eye,
> And evermore conceive some hope thereby.

In 1615 at the age of forty-three, Donne consciously turned his back on the 'sinful history of mine own youth' and was ordained a priest. From being celebrated for his erotic and sensitive love lyrics, he became one of the most noted divines and preachers of his time. Crowds thronged to church to hear his sermons. In 1623 when the new Lincoln's Inn chapel was consecrated, there was such a press of people that 'two or three were . . . taken up for dead at the time'. Inevitably, when he was appointed Dean of St Paul's in 1621 it became one of the haunts of literary London. 'St Paul's Walk,' declared John Earle in his *Microcosmographie* of 1628, 'is the land's epitome'. In fact, since the beginning of the century St Paul's had been known for its booksellers and its fashionable strollers, the 'shoal of islanders . . . swimming up and down'. It was the best place to hear the gossip from court and city. Merchants met their contacts there and bribed their spies in Whitehall. The idle passed their time by carving their names on the Cathedral's leaded roof. It contained more names, claimed the author, John Stow, modestly, 'than Stow's Chronicle'.

It was inevitable not only that the men of letters should know each other, but that they should know many of the great political, social and legal figures of the time. Many writers, after all, were also MPs, academics or clergymen; many more had done their training at one of the Inns of Court, which Ben Jonson called 'the noblest nurseries of humanity and liberty in the kingdom'. For the Inns of Court were by no means for practising lawyers only.

Donne had been there; so had Clarendon and the Cavalier poet and dramatist, John Suckling. The Inns were places of general education, where the gentry sent their sons for two or three years to learn history, music and dancing, as well as the smattering of law which would be useful for a landowner and future JP. Most of the Inns of Court men never became professional lawyers but, like Shakespeare's character, Justice Shallow, they enjoyed their student days to the full.

> I was once of Clement's Inn, where I think they will talk of mad Shallow yet. There was I, and little John Doit of Staffordshire, and black George Barnes, and Francis Pickbone, and Will Squele . . . you have not found four such swinge-bucklers in all the Inns of Court . . . Jesu, Jesu, the mad days that I have spent.

The other great meeting-place for Jonson and his 'tribe' was the Mermaid Tavern in Bread Street, where his contemporary, Fuller, described him engaging in battles of wit with Shakespeare. Jonson, Fuller wrote, was 'like a Spanish great galleon . . . built far higher in learning, solid but slow in his performances'. Shakespeare, on the other hand, he likened to 'an English man-of-war, lesser in bulk but lighter in sailing, could turn with all tides, tack about, and take advantage of all winds, by the quickness of his wit and invention'.

A tavern in seventeenth-century London was, said John Earle rather pompously, 'a degree, or if you will, a pair of stairs above an alehouse'. The diners sat at long tables and shared such dishes as beef, mutton, pigeon pie and pudding, accompanied, as Jonson knew only too well by

> . . . A pure cup of rich canary wine
> Which is the Mermaid's now but shall be mine.

Then he:

> At Bread Street's Mermaid having dined and merry,
> Proposed to go to Holborn in a wherry.

When he did go out into the streets again he would have smelled the stench of seventeenth-century London, what John Evelyn was later to call

This horrid smoke [which] obscures our churches and makes our palaces look old. It fouls our clothes and corrupts the waters, so that the very rain and refreshing dews that fall in the several seasons precipitate this impure vapour . . .

This is, perhaps, what we would notice most if we were to go back in time: the odour of tar from Blackwall mingling with the stench of the tanneries in Limehouse; the smell of the lime kilns there, and everywhere the reek of sewage. The streets were littered with sordid refuse. The Fleet River, rightly called the Ditch, was an open sewer and a hazard to health. A hundred years later the populace were still complaining of it. In 1728 in *The Dunciad* Alexander Pope was to write:

> . . . Fleet Ditch, with disemboguing streams
> Rolls the large tribute of dead dogs to Thames,
> The king of dykes! than whom no sluice of mud
> With deeper sable blots the silver flood.

The Tudors, terrified of how much the population might grow, had tried in vain to prohibit new building in the City of London. As a result, the city turned in on itself. Houses were divided and subdivided by secret doorways, back alleyways and hidden passages, each crammed with people from the cellars to the rafters. It was an ideal breeding place for plague, typhoid and smallpox, with half a million unwashed bodies packed into rotting wood and plaster houses. In the first year of James I's reign, plague did break out and swept through this mass of humanity. Those who could, fled, to the hill villages of Highgate and Hampstead, where the name of the Vale of Health perpetuates the memory of their flight. The plague spent itself before it became an epidemic but when it had passed, London life went on its unhealthy way as before. In 'the liberties', the slums outside the city walls, the hovels of the poor multiplied. It was here that the Great Plague would take its greatest toll in 1665.

THE GROWTH OF PURITANISM

᠗᠗᠗᠗᠗᠗

THE PURITAN RELIGION

By the 1630s the whole broadly based structure of the Elizabethan Church Settlement in which men could follow their individual consciences within the framework of a moderate, national church, was in danger of foundering. Charles and Laud with their authoritarian and repressive policies and their attempts to impose their idea of uniformity on the clergy, drove the Puritan element in the church into open rebellion.

Who were they, then, these Puritans? As their name suggests their aim was to 'purify' the many abuses they saw around them in the church, abuses like idleness, ignorance and pluralism among the clergy (see page 38). But they also wanted to 'purify' it from 'popish' elements, from the pernicious influence of a 'popish' court, from all the High church ceremonial which Laud sought to impose on them: fripperies like stained-glass, candlesticks and organs. John Milton, not only a great poet, but also one of the greatest of the Puritan pamphleteers, wrote:

> When the Church, without temporal support is able to do her great works upon the enforced obedience of men, it argues a divinity about her; but when she thinks to credit and better her spiritual efficacy, and to win herself respect and dread by strutting in the false vizard of worldly authority, it is evident that God is not there, but that her apostolic virtue is departed from her, and hath left her key-cold.

The Puritans rejected the idea of an ecclesiastical hierarchy, backed up, as in Laud's case, by the machinery of state and the monarch. 'We must seek into our own hearts,' wrote another pamphleteer, 'for we might have our Heaven here.' The mid-seventeenth century was, above all, a religious age. Religion was on men's lips, in their hearts and in their lives. Each man struggled daily with his conscience. Like the Nonconformist preacher, Richard Baxter, he was 'serious and solicitous about my soul's everlasting state'. The intense interest in theological controversy meant that from 1600 to 1640, nearly half the books published were on religious subjects. Merchants founded schools for the yeomen to learn to read the Bible (see plate 22); the Puritans organized travelling clergy to preach in the market-place, free from episcopal control. One of these Puritan preachers was John Bunyan who also served as a soldier in Cromwell's army. Although he would not write his principal work, *Pilgrim's Progress*, until he was jailed after the Restoration, his Puritan loyalties were forged much earlier. Unlike Milton who was a scholar and a classicist, Bunyan came of poor country stock. His writing had a homely practicality that appealed to ordinary people, along with the drama and vivid allegory of a successful preacher and the old-fashioned dignity of a man accustomed to reading his Bible. But the first part of *Pilgrim's Progress* was not published until 1678. Meanwhile, it was up to other Puritans to rally the faithful. And they did. In spite of the strict censorship laws, Puritans like William Prynne published pamphlets – nearly twenty between 1627 and 1640, all of them bitterly critical of Laud. In an age when the reading public read of little except religion, their effect was disproportionately great. For their pains, Prynne and his fellow-pamphleteers, John Lilburne and Henry Burton, were condemned to the pillory and public mutilation. 'Through these holes God can bring light to his Church!' cried Burton, pointing to the holes in the posts to which he was fastened. 'There are many hundreds which by God's assistance would willingly suffer for the cause you suffer for this day!' affirmed a woman onlooker. Such was the temper among the Puritans.

22. Seventeenth-century schoolmaster and pupils

PURITANS AND PARLIAMENT

There were many, not strictly Puritans, who espoused the Puritan cause, driven to it by Charles I's short-sighted policies. 'The truth is,' wrote George Lawson, looking back with hindsight in 1660, 'they were not unanimously resolved what they should build up, though they were agreed well enough in pulling down.' Thus, the solid, respectable country gentry despised the 'nursery of lust and intemperance' at court, while those of them who sat in Parliament had a further grudge to bear, namely Charles's high-handed attitude towards them. He had never concealed his conviction that he ruled by divine ordinance; that while Parliament could advise him, it had no right to oppose him.

> The most high and sacred order of kings, [ran the statement that Charles had the clergy read out in church] is of *divine right*, being the ordinance of God himself . . . A supreme power is given to this most excellent order by God himself in the Scriptures, which is, that kings should rule and command in their several dominions all persons of what rank or estate soever . . .

When Parliament pressed for a more assertive role in government and .dared to criticize the royal will, Charles's solution was to dissolve Parliament and refuse to call it again until it had changed its demeanour.

> Whereas . . . we have showed by our frequent meeting with our people our love to the use of Parliaments; yet the late abuse having for the present driven us out of that course, we shall account it presumption for any to prescribe any time unto us for Parliaments, the calling and continuing of which is always in our own power, and we shall be more inclinable to meet in Parliament again, when our people shall see more clearly into our intents and actions, when such as have bred this interruption shall have received their condign punishment, and those who are misled by them and by such ill reports as are raised in this occasion, shall come to a better understanding of us and themselves.

So for eleven years until 1640 Charles governed the country without calling a parliament, using as justification his theory that he ruled by 'divine right' and paying for his government by using his royal prerogative to increase taxes. Sometimes, as in the case of Ship Money, he even revived and extended old taxes. To implement his policies he relied on the help of Laud and another equally hated minister, Thomas Wentworth, Earl of Strafford.

This period did more than anything else to fire the opposition to the king. There were many who agreed with the House of Commons that even a king had to seek Parliament's consent to levy taxes. They were incensed, too, by Charles's foreign policy and the sight of the foremost Protestant prince in Europe consorting with absolutist Catholic powers. To many, Puritanism came to be identified with a healthy nationalism, while the court party represented popish, foreign ways. Slowly the king's opponents began to forget their differences in the common cause.

PURITANS IN THE NEW WORLD

Far from being repressive, the Puritans seemed to many in the seventeenth century to speak for progress. They were certainly in the vanguard of the movement to explore the New World. In 1620 a band of English and Dutch Puritans decided to cross the Atlantic and found a colony as the colonists of Virginia had done before them (see plate 23). Their ship, the 180-ton *Mayflower* (see plate 24), set sail from Plymouth in September, its sister ship, the smaller *Speedwell*, having backed out at the last minute. William Bradford, one of the Puritan leaders, described this event:

> No special leak could be found but it was judged to be the general weakness of the ship, and that she would not prove sufficient for the voyage. Upon which it was resolved to dismiss her and part of the company, and proceed with the other ship . . . And thus, like Gideon's army, this small number was divided, as if the Lord by this work of His providence thought these few too many for the great work He had to do.

The *Mayflower* sailed alone, pitting its flimsy weight against the fury of the Atlantic, and fury it was: out of sixty-seven days afloat, three-quarters were spent miserably pitching and rolling

23. Virginia in 1612; 'discribed by Captain John Smith'

in tempests and storms. There were 'many fierce storms in which the ship was shrewdly shaken,' commented Bradford laconically.

Even in normal conditions, crossing the Atlantic must have been a hideous ordeal. With no sanitation except for open boxes slung over the deck rails, the ship was an evil-smelling magnet for rats and cockroaches. The cooking, done on an iron tray covered with sand, exposed the company to constant fire risk and many of them must have wondered whether it was worth it, when confronted with the food. Spices and seasonings could do little to relieve the monotony of nine and a half weeks of dried meats, smoked fish and pickled eggs. The ship carried lemon juice as a preventive measure against scurvy but as on all seventeenth-century ships, the disease nevertheless broke out.

To the cold and sea-sick Puritans shuddering in the cramped, wet

24. *Mayflower* leaving Plymouth, 6 September 1620

ship, the one sign that they were not forgotten in their afflictions was the death of a young crew member who had mocked them. This they took to be truly the hand of God. 'Thus his curses light on his own head,' observed Bradford smugly, 'and it was an astonishment to all his fellows.'

And by now they did not have long to go. In November the first driftwood and seagulls were sighted, followed, on a cold, grey morning by the long, low shape of land (see plate 25). 'They were not a little joyful,' said Bradford, speaking for all of them – and probably not a little apprehensive too. The pioneers of the *Mayflower* were followed by other pilgrims across the Atlantic until by 1642, the Plymouth Colony and its environs numbered over 3,000 people who found there the freedom to worship as they wanted. From 1629 onwards, a further 16,000 Puritans had settled around the area of Massachusetts Bay, and from there off-shoots were established in Maine, Connecticut, Rhode Island and New Hampshire, along the Piscataqua River (see colour plate 7). New Plymouth remained a well-governed, peaceable and sturdily independent colony until it became absorbed into Massachusetts in 1691.

25. The Pilgrim Fathers reach dry land

THE INFLUENCE OF PURITANISM ON THOUGHT

On the intellectual front the Puritans also stood for progress. There was a Puritan clique among the intellectuals at Cambridge. With its questioning outlook and emphasis on individual experience, Puritanism had much in common with the new attitude to science. The scientist John Wilkins, for example, could have been talking about either discipline when he said:

> It would be much better for the commonwealth of learning if we would ground our principles rather upon the frequent experience of our own than the bare authority of others.

To other writers and intellectuals Puritanism raised new social and philosophical questions. For the first time they questioned the established social order. As early as 1602 Chapman wrote in *The Gentleman Usher*, what sounds suspiciously like a plea for republicanism:

> . . . Had all been virtuous men
> There never had been princes upon earth,
> And so no subject; all men had been princes.
> A virtuous man is subject to no prince,
> But to his soul and honour.

But equality was not what most Puritans wanted. A king might be expendable but private property was sacrosanct. When an extremist Puritan sect like Gerrard Winstanley's True Levellers, hailed by some as ancestors of our present-day communists, tried to put their ideas of equality into practice, they came up against stiff opposition. In 1649, Winstanley's followers dug up and ploughed a common in Surrey with the idea of returning the land to the people; they were interrupted by an outraged posse of local parsons and inhabitants. John Lilburne and his band of Levellers who set up what must have been the first commune in England were condemned as anarchists by Cromwell for their pains. Their crops were uprooted and their houses wrecked but no one punished their attackers: they were considered completely justified.

However, it was true that most progressive thinkers were on the Puritan side, as were 'the middling sort' – yeomen, artisans and the merchants in the towns. They were to form the backbone of the Puritan or, as it was called, Parliamentary army.

🔲🔲🔲🔲🔲

CIVIL WAR (1640-1649)

🔲🔲🔲🔲🔲

In 1639 the historian Edward Hyde, then a young lawyer, wrote:

> a small, scarce discernible cloud arose in the North, which was shortly
> after attended with such a storm, that even rooted up the greatest and
> tallest cedars of the three nations . . .

The cloud, herald of the approaching storm, appeared first in
Scotland where Charles and Laud had tried to force a new prayer
book on the unwilling Scottish Calvinists. 'Traitor! Dost thou say
Mass at my ear?' shouted an outraged Scot in St Giles's Cathedral, Edinburgh, while her fellow-countrymen in parish after
parish joined in the outcry against 'the English Popish Mass
Service Book'. Few ministers dared try to use the prayer book;
fewer still tried and succeeded. Bishop Whitford of Brechin
Cathedral conducted one uninterrupted service but with the aid
of two loaded pistols placed by him in the pulpit. When the king
overrode the protestations and insisted that his will be done, the
Scots flew to arms to defend their beloved kirk. They set out
their aims in a solemn document, the National Covenant, copies
of which were carried all over the realm for men to sign. The
Covenanters pledged themselves to uphold the Scottish service:

> We promise . . . to continue in the profession and obedience of . . .
> [our] religion; that we shall defend the same, and resist all those
> contrary errors and corruptions according to our vocation, and to the
> utmost of that power that God hath put into our hands, all the days of
> our life.

A stunned Charles was informed that to force his prayer book on the angry Scots would require an army of at least 40,000 men. To raise a force on this scale he would need a large sum of money. And to raise money on this scale, he needed Parliament.

Had Charles acted wisely, the 1640 Long Parliament could have swept away his subjects' grievances and left him on the throne. Led by John Pym, the Puritan squire from Somerset, it began as it meant to continue, with a programme of vigorous reform. Laud and Strafford, the king's two chief ministers were dismissed (Strafford was later executed); monopolies in trade granted to certain courtiers were abolished; an act was passed declaring the king's taxes, levied without consent of Parliament, unconstitutional; a further act ensured that Parliaments met every three years.

But then, faced with further reforms, Charles lost his nerve. On 4 January 1642, he stormed into the House of Commons to supervise personally the arrest of Pym and four other Members. The country prepared for war.

The country prepared for war, but there were many whose hearts cried out for peace. Lucius Cary, Viscount Falkland was one of them, representative of the sanity and reason which many on both sides longed for when they saw others of their compatriots take leave of such qualities. Clarendon has left us a famous description of Falkland's reaction to the horror of civil strife:

> From the entrance into this unnatural war his natural cheerfulness and vivacity grew clouded, and a kind of sadness and dejection of spirit stole upon him ... When there was any overture or hope of peace he would be more erect and vigorous, and exceedingly solicitous to press anything which he thought might promote it; and sitting among his friends, often, after a deep silence and frequent sighs, would, with a shrill and sad accent ingeminate the word 'Peace, peace', and would passionately profess that the very agony of the war, and the view of the calamities and desolation the kingdom did and must endure, took his sleep from him, and would shortly break his heart.

The poet, Andrew Marvell, friend and protégé of Milton, also mourned the call to arms in perhaps the loveliest poem of the Civil War:

> Unhappy! Shall we never more
> That sweet *militia* restore,
> When garlands only had their towers,
> And all the garrisons were flowers,
> When roses only arms might bear,
> And men did rosy garlands wear?

Milton himself was more intractable. Convinced Puritan that he was, he looked forward to a new England, purified by the fires of war:

> Methinks I see in my mind a noble and puissant nation rousing herself like a strong man after sleep and shaking her invincible locks. Methinks I see her as an eagle mewing her mighty youth, and kindling her undazzled eyes at the full midday beam.

But to most English families the Civil War was a time of untold misery, cutting across family and territorial loyalties. Dorothy Osborne, whose letters still survive, faced a predicament familiar to many families. Her father and brothers were strongly Royalist: her uncle was a committed Puritan and later a regicide. Her forlorn comment on hearing of a poem to be written about the war, was: 'If he [the poet] does not mingle it with a great deal of pleasing fiction, it cannot be very diverting, sure, the subject is so sad.'

The Civil War was a war of ideas and men of integrity were to be found on both sides. In general, it is true, the rural North and West were for the king, while London and the larger towns in the East supported Parliament. But in many areas yeoman fought against squire and brother took up arms against brother. Even husbands and wives could disagree. 'Two opinions,' commented John Aubrey darkly, thinking of Milton's Royalist wife, 'do not well on the same bolster.'

Some wives, however, fought gallantly alongside their husbands, holding their lands in the absence of their menfolk, even in the face of enemy siege. For two years Charlotte, Countess of

Derby, defied a Parliamentarian attempt to capture Lathom House, the Derby home. When she was relieved by a Royalist colonel, it was he who let the house fall. Charlotte, as even her enemies maintained, was 'herself the better soldier of the two'. Some families took great risks hiding fugitives in secret 'priest holes'. Others gave up their income and their lands to provide money for troops on their side. Dorothy Osborne's father, a knight with an income of £4000 a year saw it reduced to £400 before the clash of battle finally died away.

For many families, however, the war was not a matter of taking sides but simply an ordeal to be endured. They suffered grave injustice at the hands of both armies. As money ran short, the struggle became increasingly bitter and harsh methods were employed to raise additional funds. Even Lucy Hutchinson, well-born wife of a Parliamentarian colonel, did not escape such ill-treatment. She records with anger a visit by Roundhead soldiers (so called because of their habit of cropping their hair short) to her house when, having insulted her and spat at her, they made off with over £25. The ordinary people were constantly plagued by such ruffians. Some even paid a kind of protection money to keep out of trouble. Mrs Jefferies, a property owner in Hereford, listed many such payments in her account book.

> SEPTEMBER 1639: Two shillings to a strange soldier with a blue feather in his hat who said he came from Berwick.
>
> OCTOBER 1639: Fourpence to a counterfeit soldier, or a thief, rather.
>
> 1639: Five shillings to the City Militia.
>
> 1640: Two shillings to a man watching one night at Widemarsh Gate.
>
> 1642: The soldiers that shot off at my window, one shilling and beer.

In 1645, to facilitate the defence of Hereford, many of Mrs Jefferies' houses were, without warning, pulled down. Nevertheless, she was luckier than another, poorer householder, who, having seen her home demolished, was said to have died of grief.

Yet in the midst of such misery and hardship it is heartening to find that many of the lowest and poorest class were scarcely involved in the war at all. As a conflict about ideas the war was

fought among the upper and middle classes, those literate enough
to understand the fundamental differences between Anglican and
Puritan, Parliament and king. A group of soldiers patrolling the
battlefield of Marston Moor found a farm labourer in the middle
of it and warned him to leave. The king and Parliament were at
war, they explained. 'What!' was his reply. 'Has them two fallen
out then?'

This is not to say that all the common soldiers (see plate 26)
were educated and sophisticated. Nor were they all, as the leading
Parliamentarian general, Oliver Cromwell (see plate 27), said of
his troops, 'honest brave fellows that make some conscience of
what they do'. The ignorant Puritans were bigoted beyond belief:
they had merely added prejudice to their creed of credulousness
and superstition. It was not difficult for them to believe that
Charles I was the Devil and that Christ would appear on the field
of Edgehill to vanquish him. Nevertheless, theirs was a more
martial vision than that of the Royalist poet, Abraham Cowley,
who, in one poem, summoned up 10,000 cupids for the sole
purpose of scattering perfume on the battlefield. 'Think not that
the King's army is like Sodom,' the moderate Dr Fuller felt com-

26. Parliamentary soldiers: Pikeman (left) and musketeer

27. Oliver Cromwell

pelled to point out to the citizens of London in 1642, '. . . and the other army like Zion . . . no, there be drunkards on both sides, and swearers on both sides, and profane on both sides.'

There were also moderates on both sides and it was they who

28. Charles I's death warrant

felt the shock when, having defeated his forces, Parliament planned to execute its anointed king (see plate 28.). Charles I's death on a public scaffold outside his much-vaunted Banqueting House, shocked most of his countrymen. 'The blow I saw given,' said a young Londoner, 'and can truly say with a sad heart, at the instant whereof, I remember well, there was such a grone by the Thousands then present as I never heard before and desire I may never hear again.' For those who had fought for the king, the royalist poet Abraham Cowley was spokesman with a poem of despairing rage:

> Come rather Pestilence and reap us down;
> Come God's sword, rather than our own.
> Let rather *Roman* come again,
> or *Saxon*, *Norman*, or the *Dane*,
> In all the bonds we ever bore,
> We griev'd, we sigh'd, we wept; we never blusht before.

But the most eloquent epitaph was written by that gentle poet, Andrew Marvell, who, although an admirer of Cromwell's and soon to join the household of the Roundhead General Fairfax, nevertheless could not fail to be moved by the death of his king.

He nothing common did or mean
Upon that memorable Scene.
But with his keener Eye
The Axes edge did try:
Nor called the *Gods* with vulgar spight
To vindicate his helpless Right,
But bow'd his comely Head,
Down as upon a Bed.

Curiously enough, although Marvell was not there to see it, Charles did enquire about the sharpness of the executioner's axe, while a bystander remembered in particular the king's eyes which were the brightest and keenest he had ever seen them.

THE COMMONWEALTH (1649-60)

CHARLES I was dead. His two sons had fled to France and safety, the future Charles II disguised ignominiously as a servant and the fourteen-year-old James, Duke of York in the clothes of a girl – 'a mixed mohair of a light hair colour and black, and ye under-petticoat was scarlet'. The future looked bleak for the Royalists and indeed, for many of them it was, in the new republic or, to use a seventeenth-century term, new 'Commonwealth or Free State' of England.

The Roundhead victory had been a decisive one, their success being due in large measure to Oliver Cromwell who had almost singlehandedly reorganized Parliament's forces. At the battle of Edgehill in 1642, the first full-scale battle of the Civil War, the Roundhead cavalry had been routed by a single charge from the Royalists, under the command of the king's dashing and courage-ous nephew, Prince Rupert, son of his sister Elizabeth. Cromwell retired from the battlefield determined to raise and train a new cavalry force. When he met the king's forces again at Marston Moor in January 1644, the battle lasted less than two hours. Prince Rupert fled the battleground to hide ignominiously in a bean field and then was forced to retreat along a road lined with Royalist dead. But even after this victory, Cromwell was still far from satisfied. He went on to urge the creation not just of an efficient cavalry, but of a whole New Model Army. It was this army which won the decisive battle of the Civil War at Naseby (see plate 29) in Northamptonshire on 14 June 1645. Without an English army left to fight for him, Charles I was forced to attempt

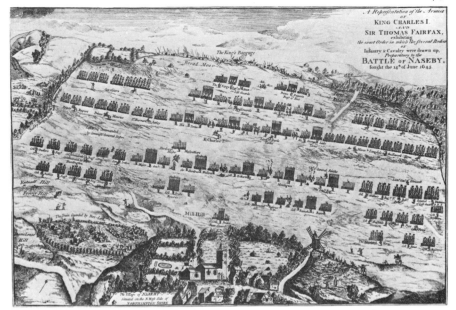

29. Contemporary engraving of the battle lines at Naseby

an alliance with the Scottish Covenanters and try to drive a wedge between them and the forces of Parliament. He might even have succeeded, had he been less high-handed and more willing to listen to the groups of Scottish ministers who came daily to plead with him to reform the church 'according to the Word of God.' As he had rightly judged, the Covenanters felt betrayed by the English Parliamentarians, who, they considered, had used them and then treated them with neglect. But in the end the disgruntled Scots withdrew, leaving the king defenceless to face the judgement of those he still called 'rebels and traitors'.

The king's supporters were also left to the mercies of their victorious enemies who levied crippling fines on their lands. Many Royalists fled, ruined, to the Continent. Many more who stayed behind had to watch the confiscation and sale of their estates. A Roundhead officer, Thomas Pride, took over the royal palace of Nonesuch; another, Charles Fleetwood, occupied Woodstock Manor. A satirical poem in 1647 chronicled the rise of this 'new gentry'.

I now have lived to see the day,
Wherein a fig-man bears such sway,
    That knights dare scarce sit by him;
Yea, I have lived to see the hour,
In which a clothier hath such power,
    That lords are glad to buy him.

Dorothy Osborne mentions the brothers and sisters of her friends condemned to languish in Parliamentarian gaols. Richard Lovelace, the Cavalier poet, was one such prisoner. He wrote one of his best poems in captivity – the chivalrous, courageous *To Althea from Prison*, which sums up all that was most honourable, loyal and enduring about the Cavalier code.

Stone walls do not a prison make
Nor iron bars a cage;
Minds innocent and quiet take
This for an hermitage;
If I have freedom in my love
And in my soul am free;
Angels alone, that soar above,
Enjoy such liberty.

What generous and gracious sentiments from a man who was to die impoverished in the Royalist cause. And indeed, many of the king's supporters did not dream of breaking their faith with him. They were pledged to avenge his memory and to serve his son. Days after his death Charles I was already achieving some sort of status as a martyr with the publication of *Eikon Basiliké* or the *Pourtraicture of His Sacred Majesty in his Solitudes and Sufferings*. This tract, almost without doubt a forgery, was supposed to have been written by the king himself during his imprisonment. It took the form of meditations, prayers and explanations of his policy and religion, and it was a powerful apologia. The Puritans tried first to suppress it and then to discredit it. Milton himself wrote a pamphlet, *Eikonoklastes*, ascribing it to a Royalist forger. The campaign was only partly successful. Even today, there are churches still standing dedicated to 'King Charles the Martyr'.

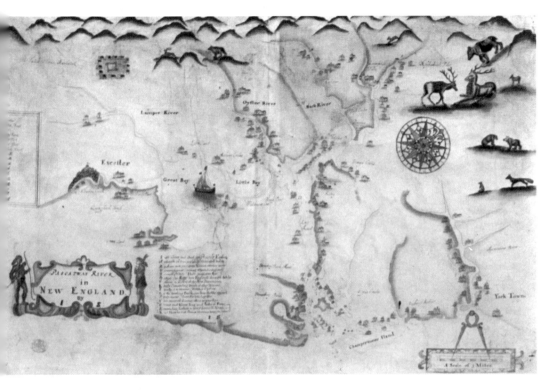

7. New Hampshire in 1612; 'discribed by Captain John Smith'

8. Charles II

9. Catharine of Braganza

But what of day-to-day life under the Commonwealth? How did it change? The traditional view is of a nation of dull, intolerant Sabbatarians, hostile to art and frightened of pleasure, however innocent. Ben Jonson's Puritans in his plays were cant-ridden drears, forever chanting, 'Very likely, exceedingly likely, very exceedingly likely'. It is true that the Puritans frowned equally on drinking and drama, the latter of which they regarded as 'the very poison and corruption of men's minds and manners'. They exacted fierce fines for the crime of breaking the Sabbath, as the parish records of St Giles's Church in London, show:

> 1641: Received of the Vintner at the Catt in Queen Street for permitting of tipling on the Lord's Day – £1-10.
>
> 1652: Received of Mr Huxley and Mr Morris, who were riding out of town in sermon time on a Fast Day – £11-.
>
> 1654: Received of William Glover in Queen Street, and of Isaac Thomas, a barber in Holborn, for trimming a beard on the Lord's Day.

The aptly named Mrs Thunder was also fined twelve shillings'for her being drunk and swearing seaven oaths'.

But the only people who suffered more than the occasional annoying restrictions, were criminals and the destitute or work-shy. Court records reveal exceptionally harsh sentences on criminals, such as the one handed out to Francis Prideaux, a thief. Not only was he whipped 'until his body be bloddy' but he was also sent to prison and fined one shilling, plus costs, a total of four shillings and eight pence in all. Puritan JPs on the whole seem to have been less sympathetic towards the unfortunate than their predecessors and it seems strange to us that the help given to the poor should have decreased. But the Puritans believed in living out St Paul's ethic: 'If any would not work, neither should he eat.'

For the rest of the population, prospects were not nearly so gloomy and life certainly not as dull as has been suggested. The Puritan government controlled the ale-houses but each village could and did provide its own merry-making – endless Church

Ales, Wakes and Bride Ales which mixed root beer and religion. Bull and bear-baiting were declared unlawful on Sundays but only so as to avoid disorder. In the meantime, it was not so hard to observe the Sabbath when there were six other days to indulge in ninepins, wrestling, bell-pulling, and playing football with pig's bladders, a sport King James had forbidden his courtiers as being 'meeter for the laming than the making able' of them. Many Puritans took pleasure in sport. John Hutchinson, the Roundhead colonel, excelled at tennis (see plate 30); Cromwell went hunting, hawking and played bowls. Many also were fond of music. There were select chamber-music recitals at the Cromwellian court. When the Protector's daughter married, the celebrations were lively enough to recall the days of the masque.

Masques did in fact take place in private houses, and plays were performed although the theatres remained obdurately closed. In 1656, however, Cromwell, swayed by his love of music, gave permission to William Davenant to reopen the theatre in Drury Lane. It presented performances with music: the first

30. Tennis court, 1658

31. Citizen and his wife in Puritan dress

English opera. Nearby and at approximately the same time, the first coffee-house opened in London.

The strictest Puritans kept to their deliberately old-fashioned mode of dress with the small, stiff ruffs of the Elizabethan era (see plate 31). But the upper classes had never subjected themselves to such mortification of the flesh. Milton and Cromwell, Eliot and Hampden all wore their hair fashionably long over their shoulders in what their more zealous – and shorn – Roundhead brethren called 'the unloveliness of love-locks'. Other rich Puritans paid fortunes for clothes and jewels. Others still, like Mrs Hutchinson, looked down on the badly dressed Puritan lower orders with a distinct lack of sisterly love.

Dorothy Osborne's letters show us how the fashionable continued to enjoy themselves under the Protectorate. On her rare visits to London, she did not observe so much that had changed. From her window in the Strand, she could still see the crowds setting off for the races; on summer evenings masked and richly dressed ladies still strolled in Hyde Park. Dorothy herself mentions going out to supper and 'play' at the newest eating-houses and vying with all the world for an audience with the famous astrologer, Lilly. She had her portrait painted by the miniaturist, Samuel Cooper; she read all the latest romances by Mademoiselle de Scudéri. 'Tis to me . . . the Prittiest,' was her verdict on one, 'and the most Naturall.' But as with people everywhere, her main preoccupation was with friends and love and marriage. She wrote wicked descriptions of current liasons in her letters.

32. The House of Commons in 1656

Wee have a lady new come in to this Country that I pity too Ex-
treamly. She is one of my Lord of Valentia's daughters and has
marryed an old fellow that is some threescore and ten whoe has a
house that is fitter for the hoggs than for her, and a fortune that will
not at all recompence the least of these inconvieniency's . . .

On one of her visits to London Dorothy mentions a plot on the
Lord Protector's life. Ironically, Cromwell had not long to live any-
way, so the risk the plotters took was unnecessary. In September
1658 he died and the unity of the Commonwealth died with him.
Squabbling broke out between Parliament (see plate 32) and the
Parliamentarian army and in the autumn of 1659 the army dissolved Parliament by force. The restoration of the monarchy
seemed to some leaders the only way to avoid anarchy and return
to stable government. They made overtures to Charles II and he
went out of his way to respond, promising 'liberty to tender
conscience' (that is, freedom of worship, to the Puritans). By this
action, his reinstatement was assured. By May 1660 the country
knew that they were to have another king. The glorious experiment of the 'Free State' of England, of civil liberty and righteous
government, was over. Milton spoke for many when, in the words
of Samson in *Samson Agonistes*, he said:

> Now blind, dishearten'd, sham'd, dishonour'd, quell'd,
> To what can I be useful, wherein serve
> My nation . . .

⊠⊠⊠⊠⊠

LIFE AFTER THE RESTORATION

⊠⊠⊠⊠⊠

ON 1 January 1660, a twenty-seven-year-old Londoner decided to keep a diary.

> I live in Axe-yard, [wrote Samuel Pepys,] having my wife and servant Jane, and no more in family than us three . . . The condition of the State was thus . . .

So begins one of the most candid, absorbing, highly personal, yet generally illuminating of journals. So also begins a period uniquely rich in documentation. The late seventeenth century was a time when many Englishmen kept diaries or wrote memoirs. Besides Pepys himself, there were John Evelyn and the intrepid lady traveller, Celia Fiennes. Together with the racy memoirs of a French aristocrat, the Comte de Grammont, transcribed by his brother-in-law, Anthony Hamilton, another luminary at Charles II's court, they give a vivid picture of English life after the Restoration.

Of the diarists John Evelyn was the most pious and straitlaced, but even he could not fail to reflect the joy and hope felt by almost every Englishman, and especially every Londoner, at Charles II's Restoration.

THE COURTS

Charles II (1660–85)

The reinstated king landed at Dover on 23 May 1660. He entered London in full splendour on his thirtieth birthday, 29 May. Evelyn was one of the wildly cheering Londoners who greeted his triumphant arrival

With . . . above 2000 horse and foot, brandishing their swords and shouting with inexpressible joy; the ways strewed with flowers, the bells ringing, the streets hung with tapestry, fountains running with wine; the Mayor, aldermen, all the companies in their liveries, chains of gold, banners; lords and nobles, cloth of silver, gold and velvet everybody clad in, the windows and balconies all set with ladies, trumpets, music and myriads of people flocking the streets . . . I stood in the Strand and beheld it, and blessed God.

Such rejoicing may seem strange in a city which had supported Parliament in the Civil War. But after the strife and conflict of the previous three decades, the spirit of compromise was in the air. The people of England had learnt the value of tolerance from having seen and lived through the disastrous effects of confrontation. They had learnt too a new reverence for freedom of thought and conscience.

But if there was a desire for unity and compromise, it was not a servile one. Above all, they were not prepared to renounce the hard-won power of Parliament or underestimate the part it was to play in shaping the future of the nation. 'A free Parliament! A free Parliament!' shouted the crowds in Threadneedle Street to which their new monarch sensibly replied, 'Pray be quiet, ye shall have a free Parliament.'

Much of Charles's popularity lay in his skill in recognizing the need to compromise. He was the first of the Stuarts to do so. From the start, he made it clear that he was determined not to repeat the mistakes of his father's reign. The tactful and generous Act of Indemnity and Oblivion forgave his enemies and wiped the slate clean. Only the regicides, those who had signed his father's death-warrant, were called to account (see plate 33), and in the end not even all of them paid the penalty. 'I confess I am weary of hanging – let it sleep,' scribbled Charles, passing their reprieve across the council table to one of his ministers, Edward Hyde. Good-humouredly it was said that he joked that it had been his own fault that he had been absent so long, for he saw nobody that did not protest he had ever wished for his return. And indeed, for at least the first ten years of his reign the old and bitter divisions between

33. The execution of the regicides, 1660

court and country collapsed. The whole of the gentle class were
his potential courtiers and supporters. The 1661 Parliament was
called the Cavalier Parliament after its predominant monarchists.
All England flocked to wait on the king at Whitehall. 'Whitehall
is like a fair all day,' commented a disgruntled squire.

Genial and accessible, Charles II was an easy monarch to love.
A contemporary said he liked 'to be easy himself and to make
everybody else so'. Such was his character that he effortlessly
embodied the compromising spirit of the age. To the end of his
reign this virtue outweighed his faults in the minds of his subjects. To the common people, hungering for glamour after the
sobriety of the Commonwealth, he was an attractive figure (see
colour plate 8), tall and dashing, 'a sauntering prince', dignified
yet courteous and generous to those around him. His six weeks as
a fugitive after the Battle of Worcester had taught him to be at
ease with his subjects from any walk of life. This period had also
earned him his nickname – 'The Black Boy' from his swarthy
appearance. In 1651 the Parliamentary 'Wanted' notices ran:
'Wanted – a tall, black man, six foot two inches high.'

Yet for all his casual charm, Charles's court was an elegant and
graceful one. He brought French culture and French manners
back from Versailles, the glittering palace of Louis XIV, the Sun
King. Among the innovations were French fashions and French

cuisine. Chatelin's in Covent Garden served ragoût (a French stew) and salads to spendthrift courtiers. Fashionable ladies flocked to Parisian *modistes* for the current look of rich *déshabille*. Charles himself pestered his sister Minette in France to send him the new Persian vest waistcoats which Louis had adopted. When they arrived, he dressed his valets in them, much to Louis' fury. French furniture too became the rage. In 1669 the English Ambassador in Paris counted 4000 gilt mirrors sent to England in a single summer. More useful were the tiny silver brushes imported for the courtiers to use to clean their teeth, and the first sedan chairs, a new mode of transport in Paris. The king was an enthusiastic patron of good taste and 'good breading', the lack of which, as he wrote sadly to his sister, was 'a disease very much spread over this country'.

Like his father he considered it both a pleasure and a duty to patronize the arts. He was, said Evelyn, a king who 'loved planting and building and brought in a polite way of living'. He set to work immediately to restore the glories of Whitehall, stripped and looted during the war years. As early as June 1660, Evelyn was noting in his diary that, 'Goods that had been pillaged . . . were now daily brought in, and restored upon proclamation; as plate, hangings, pictures, etc.' They included pictures which Charles would never have been able to afford to buy: 'divers of the best pictures of the great masters, Raphael, Titian, etc.' Alongside them were hung pictures by living artists, in particular, the richly draped portraits of Sir Peter Lely. Lely, portrait painter to Charles II, was the first painter to attain anything like his predecessor, Van Dyck's, eminence. He lacked the individualistic creative genius of Van Dyck but his voluptuous portraits of court beauties in their silks and satins accurately mirrored Charles II's age.

Charles's library, too, was restocked with beautifully bound and illuminated books for a king who liked to look at and handle precious things, but not to read. Even in his private chapel, the rich ceremonial trappings gradually reappeared and for once the Puritan sensibilities of London were not offended. On the contrary, they flocked to gaze at the crimson cushions and cloth of gold among which the king said his Sunday morning prayers. Such was Charles's real and universal popularity.

Throughout his reign Charles could not build as he would have liked to, so hampered was he by an empty Treasury and a host of claimants, victims of the late war, eager to prey upon his generous nature. Instead, wisely, he concentrated on restoring his largest palaces, and he was lucky to have Christopher Wren, the young Assistant Surveyor-General (see plate 34), to help him. Charles had made the post of Surveyor-General into a political appointment and awarded it to Sir John Denham, the Cavalier poet, as a sign of his gratitude. Fortunately, Wren bore the brunt of the work. Indeed, Denham was so inexperienced that in 1661 he had to be dissuaded from building the new wing of Tudor Greenwich on piles on the river bank. Instead, John Webb's King Charles II

34. Sir Christopher Wren

block began to rise at a safe distance from the Thames. At Windsor the new rooms were decorated with the magical wood-carvings of Grinling Gibbons, John Evelyn's protégé. The Chapel and part of St George's Hall were covered in magnificent murals, the work of the Italian painter, Antonio Verrio.

Windsor also reflected Charles II's love of parks and gardening. Evelyn, himself a keen gardener, went especially to admire it:

> There was now the terrace brought almost round the old Castle, the grass made clean, even, and curiously turfed; the avenues to the new park, and other walks, planted with elms and limes, and a pretty canal, and receptacle for fowl . . .

In St James's Park in London, too, the king repaired the neglect, replanted trees and stocked the pond with waterfowl, including a crane with a jointed wooden leg made, according to Evelyn, by an old soldier. The king went daily to feed the ducks in public, bowing and taking off his hat to greet his subjects. And all over the country his subjects followed his example, planting gardens, laying out parks, rebuilding and restoring their scarred and shattered houses. This was to be one of Charles's greatest legacies.

Another was his interest in science, an interest which led to his patronage of the Royal Society, which met first on an informal basis in Christopher Wren's rooms at Gresham College. He encouraged a love of music, went regularly to the theatre and granted a Royal Charter to the Philosophical Society, staying up all night to watch the eclipse of Saturn with them, through a telescope.

But his interests were not all so learned nor did he totally escape criticism, the more so as his reign progressed and the euphoria of the Restoration inevitably wore thin. There were many who were shocked by his casual morals and easy-going way of life: by a king who could read important dispatches booted and spurred and then ride off blithely for a day's carefree hunting; by a king determined not to let affairs of state mar one moment of his pleasure, be it tennis, swimming, riding or escaping from his courtiers to eat cherries in the depths of Epping forest. In fact,

Charles was probably guilty of having too many interests rather than of deliberate neglectfulness. He rose every day at five, no matter what time he had retired the night before. But the criticism persisted as did the scandal about his mistresses (see plate 35), for whom he had largely forsaken Catherine of Braganza, his buck-toothed queen (see colour plate 9). She, poor lady, was deeply in

Barbara Castlemaine

Nell Gwynne

Lucy Walter

Louise de Kéroualle

35. Charles I's mistresses

love with her handsome husband and suffered torments of jealousy. But it was a marriage of diplomatic convenience only. Try as she might, Catherine did not appeal to Charles, who had the pick of the most beautiful and sophisticated women in England. She did not even have any children to console her: it was a barren union and although Charles had numerous illegitimate children, he never had a legitimate heir. The queen who was Portuguese and could speak scarcely a word of English, faded more and more into the background, forced to be content with watching her rivals occupy the centre of the stage. Nevertheless, her husband, when he saw her, treated her with courtly deference, unlike some of the heartless gallants at court who laughed at her and her Portuguese ladies-in-waiting behind their backs. Not only, it was said, were they all extremely ugly, but they suffered from an excess of Catholic modesty. It was a standing joke at court that they refused to sleep in a bed where a man had slept before them.

And so Charles looked elsewhere for feminine company. Startled Whitehall sentries met their master in the early mornings returning to his lodgings after having paid a visit to his celebrated mistress, Barbara Castlemaine. It was a common sight in London to see 'the King chatting familiarly in the park with Nelly [Gwynne] as she leaned over her garden wall above the Mall'. Pious John Evelyn was shocked by the intimate candlelit court supper parties, and the sight of La Castlemaine marrying off her flagrantly illegitimate daughters in gold and silver lace. The king, so went the current scandal, paid attention only to his mistresses, while his mother, Charles I's widow, and her advisers governed the country.

In the light of such speculation about who really ruled, the old spectre of popery inevitably resurrected itself. After all, no Englishman could forget that the king's mother, Henrietta Maria was a Frenchwoman and a devout Roman Catholic. So too was the heir to the throne, his brother, James, Duke of York, who had been converted even before he married the bigotedly Catholic Italian princess, Mary of Modena. It was as if the clock had been put back thirty years. The flames of anti-popery were fuelled afresh. But it was James who was the target for the fear and hatred of the people. In his reign the blaze would re-ignite itself. Meanwhile, while Charles ruled he sat fairly securely if not firmly on the throne. He had, in the end, the real affection of the majority of his subjects. 'So pleasant a man,' ran the verdict of one, 'that no one could be sorrowful under his government.' There were many who thought the same when the fifty-four-year-old king suffered a stroke and died suddenly in 1685. They looked forward with foreboding to the accession of his brother.

James II (1685–8)

If Charles II was excused his faults, James II (see plate 36) was given credit for none of his virtues. He was less spendthrift, more honest and stubbornly loyal than any other Stuart king. Unfortunately, however, his loyalties lay in the wrong direction. 'This prince,' Lauderdale had written of him in 1679, 'has all the weakness of his father without his strength . . . He is as very a papist as the pope himself, which will be his ruin . . .' Like his father, James had a rigid belief in the divine nature of kingship but, if anything, he was the more obstinate and narrow-minded of the two. He blamed Charles I's downfall not on his inability to compromise but on the fact that he had made any concessions at all. To James his opponents were all 'knaves', 'rogues', 'aetheists' and 'cattle', or, the worst insult of all to such an opinionated king, 'republicans'. On a personal level, James lacked his father's dignity or his brother's grace and charm. He found it difficult to communicate even with the people he knew best at court. The memoirs of de Grammont have left us a wickedly funny account of the king's clumsy approaches to a would-be royal mistress:

> He entertained her with what he had in his head; telling her miracles of the cunning of foxes and the mettle of horses; giving her accounts of broken legs and arms, dislocated shoulders, and other curious . . . adventures.

No wonder the witty Charles II had treated his brother as somewhat of a royal joke, declaring that James's mistresses were so

36. James II by Sir Godfrey Kneller

ugly they were clearly imposed on him as some kind of penance.

James's queen, on the other hand, was famous for her beauty, but lacked the sensuality that the king looked for and found in other less decorative women. 'She has no other amusements whatsoever,' wrote a contemporary, 'save that of playing basset every evening – except on Sundays and the eve of days on which she receives communion.' Mary was twenty-five years younger than her husband and he tended to treat her like an innocent child. On her behalf he tried to impose a new morality in lax Whitehall. Even the Duke of St Albans, illegitimate son of Charles II, was publicly rebuked for having 'the impudence to appear drunk in the Queen's presence'. But in spite of his efforts, Mary of Modena never came to like Whitehall which she called 'one of the largest and most uncomfortable houses in the world'. She preferred Richmond Palace for which Wren was instructed to draw up new plans, although James II was no longer king by the time work was started. In Whitehall itself the queen's apartments were redecorated, testimony to the fact that Charles's wife had lived far less splendidly than his rapacious mistresses. Evelyn, as always a connoisseur, admired the costly hangings on Mary's bed and the 'incomparable' Gibbons carving about the chimney-piece. In the queen's new Catholic chapel Gibbons's carvings in white marble vied with the magnificent Verrio frescoes on the ceiling. Again, Evelyn could not help but admire it, although as a stout Protestant he disapproved of popery. He was horrified when a mere four days after his accession, the new king publicly celebrated the Mass.

> He, to the good grief of his subjects, did now, for the first time, go to mass publicly, the doors being set wide open . . . I could not believe that I would ever have seen such things in the King of England's palace, after it had pleased God to enlighten this nation.

Others too were shocked. At court there was constant bickering between Catholics and Protestants. Many of the Protestant nobility deliberately stayed away, in spite of James's pathetic efforts to maintain the brilliance which had characterized his brother's court. A reception for the king's birthday on 14 October was

10. The Great Fire of London, 1666

11. Mausoleum at Castle Howard, Yorkshire

12. Castle Howard

embarrassingly ill-attended. In the previous reign, as James II well knew, such an occasion would have attracted a vast and eager crowd.

James's one halcyon period of popularity was ominously short-lived – the result of a resurgence of loyalty to the Crown after he had defeated an armed rebellion in the west country in 1685. On June 11, James, Duke of Monmouth landed at Lyme Regis with a force of 150 followers and publicly proclaimed himself King of England. In fact, he was of royal blood – the eldest bastard son of Charles II, born while the king was in exile, to his mistress, Lucy Walter. Monmouth was charming, intelligent and handsome but easily led and as a result widely mistrusted. At any rate, he could not carry even the people of the west country with him. He collected a sizeable but miserably under-equipped army and tried in vain to gain admittance to the city of Bristol. On July 5 he was defeated and taken prisoner by James's forces at the night battle of Sedgemoor. A short time afterwards, he was executed. Besides this execution which was probably justified, James did much to sour his success by countenancing a vindictive vendetta of revenge in the west. In Judge Jeffreys' notorious 'Bloody Assizes', two to three hundred of his subjects were put to death, many more flogged and approximately eight hundred deported to the West Indies. Daily reports were sent back to the king who tactlessly described the tyranny as his 'campaign in the West'.

In the circumstances, the king's delight in military matters alarmed his increasingly uneasy subjects. The courtiers tired of his constant reviews of his troops and the favour shown to his beloved military. The people were suspicious of the very efficiency of the army and feared that it would be used against them and for the Pope. One of the popular rhymes of the time illustrates this fear:

> Now pause, and view the Army Royal
> Compos'd of valiant souls and loyal
> Not rais'd (as ill men say) to hurt ye
> But to defend, or to convert ye.

Their fears were exacerbated by reports of the favour shown to the Papal Nuncio at court. In 1687 the king and queen openly knelt to receive his blessing. Public reaction was instantaneous and indignant. Why should the king of England kneel to the representative of a mere bishop of Rome?

Nevertheless, the people could allay their fears with the thought that when James died, the Protestant succession was assured. When he married the Catholic princess, Mary of Modena, James was already a widower with two daughters by his first marriage who had been brought up in the Protestant faith. Anne Hyde, his first wife, was the daughter of Charles II's minister, Edward Hyde, Earl of Clarendon. James had seduced her when he was still Duke of York, and when she became pregnant, agreed to marry her. Anne Hyde died in 1671 after she, too, had been converted to Catholicism: indeed, it was her conversion which probably influenced James's. However, her two daughters, Mary, aged nine, and six-year-old Anne, grew up as Protestants. Mary, moreover, married the foremost Protestant ruler in Europe, the Dutch prince, William of Orange. Thus, secure in the knowledge that a Protestant princess was next in line to the throne, the English people might well have felt able to put up with James while he lived. But in 1687 something happened which radically changed the future outlook: after several miscarriages, Mary of Modena once again became pregnant, and this time succeeded in giving birth to a son and heir. 'A young prince born,' wrote Evelyn, 'which will cause disputes.' And indeed, the prospect of a Catholic dynasty was not one which many Englishmen could endure. Nor could James's daughters, hitherto loyal to their father.

Nevertheless, the bloodless 'revolution' which forced James II to abdicate in favour of his daughter Mary was by no means a national revolt, although the country generally was probably in sympathy with its aims. Seven people only signed the petition asking William to intervene and they were mostly noblemen with personal grudges to bear against a papist, French-loving king. They appealed to William because he was the husband of the Protestant heir to the throne and because Mary had all along insisted that she would only rule England jointly with him.

Together husband and wife convinced themselves that it was their duty to save England from becoming a province of Rome. But when William's army landed in the west country in November 1688, there was still an anointed king on the English throne. James was not about to abdicate willingly even for his eldest daughter. Moreover, the temper of the people was uncertain. There was a real possibility that William's arrival might provoke another civil war. In the end William's military astuteness and James's moral collapse decided the day. Cleverly, the Prince of Orange avoided direct confrontation with the king's forces but slowly and relentlessly drove on towards London while James's army, unwilling to fight, retreated before him. When it came to it, the people of England were not prepared to fight for James. One by one his supporters fell by the wayside or actively changed masters. Thus abandoned, James fell back on his Catholic counsellors and his wife. 'The Virgin Mary is to do all,' commented a contemporary sarcastically, effectively summing up the atmosphere of general helplessness at Whitehall. On 10 December 1688, the queen fled, taking the infant Prince of Wales with her to France and safety. Even her son's legitimacy was in doubt, the result of a clever rumour spread by the king's opponents. James himself was so inept that he could not manage a successful escape until William tactfully gave him the chance. By the end of the year, he had joined his wife in France. 'When you listen to him [talk],' so ran the saying among the wits of the French court, 'you realize why he is here.'

William (1689–1702) and Mary (1689–94)

It poured with rain on the day William of Orange made his ceremonial entry into London. Yet the streets were crowded with Londoners, anxious to catch a glimpse of the heroic saviour of the Protestant faith. They were disappointed. Characteristically, for a man who, as Bishop Burnet said, 'neither loved shows nor shouting', the new king travelled in a closed carriage by a secret route. William never courted popularity; indeed, he went out of his way to guard his privacy and it was his wife, Mary, who gained

37 and 38. William and Mary

the love of the populace in this 'double-bottomed monarchy'.

She entered her new kingdom with more pleasing pomp and spectacle, sailing up the river to Whitehall with a large and colourful retinue on May 26. There Lady Churchill saw her happily exploring every room like any newly settled housewife, 'looking into every closet and conveniency and turning up the quilts of the beds just as people do at an inn'. There were those who disapproved of her unconcealed pleasure at her new position. 'I thought a little more seriousness had done as well,' Burnet wrote critically, 'when she came into her father's Palace and was to be sat on his throne the next day.'

But among those who watched the royal couple process from Whitehall to the Banqueting House where Lords and Commons duly proclaimed them king and queen, there was no doubt who was the more attractive figure. Six feet tall, handsome and, at twenty-six, glowing with health and cheerfulness, Queen Mary offered a significant contrast to her stunted, irritable and sickly husband. And indeed, so disappointed had she been when Charles II, to please the Protestants, chose this taciturn asthmatic to marry her, that she burst into tears and cried all the way through the wedding ceremony. But her aversion did not last. Mary was an emotional and affectionate woman, who managed to penetrate her husband's reserve and show him the admiration and understanding that he needed. In Holland she had seen the devotion he inspired in those who served him and heard of his qualities as a fearless leader in the field of battle. As a result, it was she who first fell in love with William and gave him far more loyalty than he ever gave her. As a newly married teenager, she was not mature or clever enough for him to regard her as an equal, and it was his mistress, Elizabeth Villiers, who was a real companion to the warrior-king. In spite of his neglect, Mary's affection never faltered. Ever eager to please him, she slavishly pandered to his autocratic notions of wifely duty. Although she was the true heir, there was never any question of an undivided monarchy. From the beginning Mary assumed that William would rule jointly with her.

At the start of their joint reign, William made the decisions as he always had done. But during his annual absences on military campaigns, Mary was forced to take a more active part in government. Once she had gained confidence, she began to assert herself and became more than a decorative figurehead at Council meetings, eventually earning the respect of her Councillors for her sound and impartial judgement.

In each of their six years' joint rule, William spent six months with his army. Spring and summer were to William the natural campaigning seasons, just as they had been hunting seasons to Mary's great-grandfather, James I. On the very day of his coronation, news had come that the deposed King James II had gathered an army in France and raised his standard in Ireland in a futile attempt to win back his throne. Having routed James in Ireland, William was still faced with the French in Europe: for years the Protestant Dutch and the Catholic French had been embroiled in a bitter and costly war. For many young Englishmen, 'the gentlemen who combed their flowing wigs and exchanged their richly perfumed snuffs at the St James's coffeehouses', it was an exciting adventure to follow their new king into battle. But others regarded the war as a purely Dutch affair and resented England being dragged into it. They saw it as a waste of English blood and English money.

Indeed, William's eagerness to defend his homeland and devotion to things Dutch met with fierce criticism among many of his subjects. The Whitehall courtiers, in particular, resented his private supper parties, drinking Dutch gin with Dutch friends, the only time, it was said, when he forgot to be taciturn, and relaxed. Many of these friends had been ennobled with English titles: Arnoud van Keppel was created Earl of Albermarle; the unpopular Bentinck became Earl of Portland. He also became immensely rich as William lavished sinecures on him, but remained notoriously stingy and stand-offish, well deserving his nickname, 'the Wooden Man'. A lampoon of the time mocked his supposed hold over the king:

> Then Benting up-locks
> His King in a box
> And you see him no more till supper.

William was too strong-willed for Bentinck's influence to have been serious and in any case, it did not take Bentinck to make him ungregarious. Upon his arrival in Whitehall, he cast a pall of gloom over the once scintillating English court, shunning social occasions and preferring to work alone in his closet. In a way he was right to hold himself aloof from the endlessly conniving noble factions, most of whom, as he was well aware, 'looked one way and rowed another' – that is, across the water to the House of Stuart. But his refusal to allow his wife to hold any brilliant receptions meant that he missed his chance of forming any sort of bond with his courtiers. He was 'not easily come at, nor spoke to', commented Bishop Burnet meaningfully.

So much did William dislike Whitehall that in due time he refused to live there, on the grounds that the damp river mists were bad for his asthmatic chest. In fact, he saw in Wolsey's old palace of Hampton Court, the chance to live a retiring life away from London, as well as the ideal site for a new and splendid palace, rivalling Versailles in its magnificence. Although parsimonious in other things, William never stinted on building works or his army, and Christopher Wren, since 1669 the Surveyor-General, was given an extensive brief. He began by making the dark, cramped Tudor rooms temporarily habitable, replacing the mullioned glass with what were probably the first sash windows seen in England. The queen's suite of rooms in the Water Gallery were remodelled and redecorated by the superb craftsmen representative of the flowering of art in the late Stuart era. On the ceilings, with subtle flattery, Verrio painted English kings and queens mingling with the gods of Olympus. On the walls, Grinling Gibbons carved abundant, lifelike swags of flowers and fruit. The Dutch designer, Daniel Marot, was responsible for the most Dutch of all the rooms in the queen's apartments: the Delft-ware closet, built to house Mary's growing collection of blue and white china. The queen's hobby started a craze among English collectors so that Daniel Defoe, in his *Tour of Great Britain*, mocked her ardent imitators slavishly 'piling their China upon the Tops of Cabinets, Scrutores, and every Chymncy-Piece, to the Tops of the Ceilings'. But the covetous Evelyn was duly impressed by 'the Queen's rare cabinets and collections of china', which, he wrote in July 1693, 'was wonderfully rich and plentiful especially a large cabinet, looking-glass frame and stands, all of amber, much of it white . . . esteemed worth £4000.' Mary's oriental cabinets were imported by the East India Company, as were the chintzes and painted calicos she favoured for covering furniture and curtaining beds. So disastrous was the effect of this preference upon English manufacturers that in the end an act had to be passed prohibiting the import and sale of foreign materials. But other fashions the queen set were less harmful, indeed sometimes beneficial. Unusually for the period, she had built herself 'a small Bathing-Room, made very fine, suited to either hot or cold Bathing, as the Season should invite.' Sadly, it is no longer there for us to see – when Wren's wings were finished (see plate 39), the queen's old apartments were demolished – but the example was duly noted by many of those building new country houses. Aristocratic ladies also copied her homely pastimes like knotting fringe or embroidery and affected to love the small pug dogs which were the trademark of the family of Orange.

While the king was away, his queen lived a hard-working and solitary life. She rose at six and in a full day one of her few

39. Fountain Court, Hampton Court Palace, by Sir Christopher Wren

relaxations was a hurried game of cards. Evenings were set aside for
the sacred ritual of her daily letter to the king, couched in terms of
such humility that it is hard to believe that it was her consort she
was writing to. Her greatest pleasure, apart from his company,
was to discuss the progress of the building works with Wren. 'The
indefatigable Queen Mary,' commented Nicholas Hawksmoor,
Wren's assistant, 'was constantly at his elbow . . . with most
determined ideas.' Her greatest contribution was in the gardens
where she complemented the magnificent façades now rising with
sweeping avenues, 'great fountaines and grass plotts and gravell

walks'. In her passion for gardening she built massive hot-houses and filled them with luxuriant tropical plants sent from Virginia, the West Indies and the Canary Islands.

Parliament was ill pleased by both its monarchs' isolation and their extravagance. To wheedle the necessary money from the worthy Members, William had to compromise and move closer to London. In due course, he bought Lord Nottingham's gracious country house in Kensington, the present Kensington Palace, then a village separated from Whitehall by fields and woods. Wren's brief was to convert this into a family home for William and Mary. There were to be no grand reception rooms, suitable for large-scale entertaining. It was to prove fortunate that William ever bought it. In 1691 a disastrous fire gutted much of the Palace of Whitehall. Seven years later, another fire destroyed it altogether.

Meanwhile, work at Hampton Court progressed slowly and fitfully. It was nowhere near completion when the queen died of smallpox at Kensington in the winter of 1694. 'Just the shell up', was all Celia Fiennes saw when she visited it, 'and some of the Rooms of State ceil'd but nothing finished.' The delay had been yet another disappointment to the thirty-two-year-old queen whose last few years had been marred by bitterness. Prematurely old and fat, perhaps because of her excessive liking for Dutch butter and Dutch chocolate, she had longed in vain for a child. Two miscarriages early in her married life had given her at least some hope that she might conceive again. 'I know the Lord might still give me one [a son]', she wrote in her journal, 'if it seemed good to Him.' As she grew older and lost hope, a cloud fell on her relationship with Anne, her younger sister, who, for the time being at least, had a son and heir, the frail and sickly Duke of Gloucester, until he succumbed to a fatal disease in the summer of 1700. A quarrel broke out over Anne's domineering friend, Sarah Churchill, wife of John Churchill, future Duke of Marl-borough and victor of Blenheim. When Mary ordered Sarah dis-missed from court, Anne retired to Sion House and never spoke to her sister again.

But if Mary's sister did not grieve for her, her husband was prostrated, although while she lived he had shown her only grudging and cursory attention. William wept; he prayed; he fainted and was carried swooning from her bedroom; he cut off a lock of her hair and henceforth carried it next to his heart. In this strange man such sorrow was probably quite genuine but it was allied to uncertainty: he did not know if he could continue to rule alone. Wisely, he gave his popular queen a splendid funeral and in her memory ordered Wren to resume work on her favourite project – the conversion of the old Palace of Greenwich into a seamen's hospital (see plate 40).

In fact, there was no move to unseat him. The king had gained the respect of Parliament, if not their love. He ruled on alone and alone he watched his life's dream, the great palace of Hampton Court, completed by Wren. But he took no joy in it according to a contemporary who saw the king's wizened figure hobbling through the splendid gold and crimson rooms. Nor did he make use of all this space and splendour for entertainments. The king's only social activity now was drinking, and this, only with his cronies.

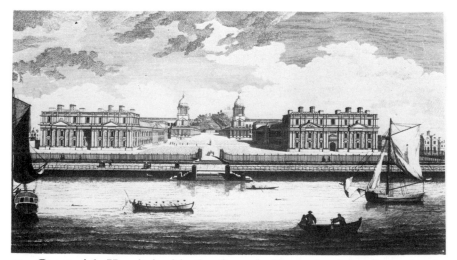

40. Greenwich Hospital with the Queen's House by Inigo Jones in the centre, John Webb's King Charles II block in the foreground and Wren's new buildings in between

In the spring of 1702 he was riding in the park at Hampton when he was thrown from his horse and, landing clumsily, broke his collar-bone. A coach bore him to the more informal atmosphere and friendlier surroundings of Kensington and it was there that he died a few weeks later at the age of fifty-one. He had never understood his English subjects and they, in turn, had never warmed to him. The funeral of this unloveable and taciturn king was, said Bishop Burnet, 'scarse decent'.

41. Queen Anne with her son, William, Duke of Gloucester

Anne (1702–14)

The last sovereign of the House of Stuart bore no resemblance to the rest of her family. Plump, plain and simple, Queen Anne took after her mother's family, the Hydes (see plate 41). Her defects were shared by her bovine and drunken husband, Prince George of Denmark, who in twenty years of living in England never mastered his adopted country's language. A popular rhyme of the reign reflected their mutual passion for food and drink:

> King William thinks all,
> Queen Mary talks all,
> Prince George drinks all,
> And Princess Anne eats all.

Yet it was a happy if unexciting marriage. Prince George was too indolent to be unfaithful to his wife. Their union was marred only by the desperate struggle to produce an heir. Every year from 1683 to 1700, the queen duly became pregnant and with equal and tragic inevitability, all but one of her seventeen children miscarried, were still-born or died. The final blow came with the death in 1700 of the young Duke of Gloucester. In an agony of grief, the queen saw it as punishment for her sins in betraying her father, King James.

Now the heir to the Protestant succession was James I's grandchild, Sophia, Electress of Hanover, daughter of Charles I's much-loved sister, Elizabeth. She was never to sit on the English throne – she died in 1714 two months before Anne – but at least she was blessed with a strong and healthy son, the future King George I, who inherited his mother's claim on her death. It was a measure of how far the country had turned against the papist James II and his family that they were prepared, when Anne died, to accept a German as king. Anne, however, felt nothing but resentment for her foreign heirs and, while she lived, refused to allow them entry into England. Possibly her antipathy sprang from the fact that George of Hanover had once sought her hand in marriage and then backed out, leaving the way free for George of Denmark.

The royal couple, in the eight or so years left to them, lived a routine and retiring life, moving from palace to palace according to a strict yearly programme. Kensington was their favourite among the royal residences because it was the most homely, but even so Anne built herself a glorified cottage on the boundaries of Windsor Park where she could totally relax – 'a little retreate out of the Palace', according to Celia Fiennes. With her feminine eye for detail, Celia Fiennes admired the crimson and white damask upholstery and the 'little wanscoate tables for tea, cards or writeing'. She was also impressed by a feature of the queen's dressing-room – 'a closet that leads to a little place with a seat of easement of marble with sluices of water to wash all down'.

But in an age of incomparable architects, Anne was not interested in commissioning grandiose royal buildings. 'She was never expensive, nor made any foolish buildings,' judged the Duchess of Marlborough with sublime disregard for her own ruinously expensive works at Blenheim Palace. Wren was engaged to build an orangery at Kensington. The queen, wrote Defoe, 'was often pleased to make the Green House, which is very beautiful, her Summer Supper House.' But this apart, her only contribution to seventeenth-century architecture was some very necessary repair work at Windsor, untouched since Charles II's reign.

The arts, too, suffered. Godfrey Kneller, appointed the court Principal Painter in 1691, has been said to reflect the taste of three sovereigns with no interest in the arts. The last of these sovereigns, George I, was perhaps the least art-loving monarch England has ever had: it was he who created Kneller a baronet. When Kneller died in 1723, he left in his studio eight hundred unfinished pictures, telling evidence of his commercial attitude to painting. He could, on occasion, prove himself a superb draughtsman and colourist, but all too often in his hurry to execute all his commissions, his work was slipshod and careless. He seldom varied the stock designs for portraits which he had inherited from Lely and rarely was he interested enough to experiment with colour. With the help of his assistants who sketched in the accessories – an accepted practice which Lely, too, had taken advantage of – he painted almost every eminent personality of the day. Portraits rolled out of the Kneller studio as if on an artistic production line: between 1702 and 1714, for example, he painted the famous series of forty-two portraits of the rich and cultivated members of the Kit-Kat Club, now hanging in the National Portrait Gallery. The standard is uneven, to say the least. Nevertheless, some of Kneller's work reveals a desire to see beyond the bland face of his sitter and give an impression of character, however unflattering. That it often was, can be seen in his portrait of the writer, Pope, whose bitterness shows plainly in his face for all the world to see.

If she did not patronize the arts, Queen Anne did take an interest in the royal gardens, laying out new lawns and walks and enthusiastically planting trees. At Kensington she converted a disused gravel-pit into such a lovely garden that even the habitually critical Addison was forced to observe: 'It must have been a fine genius for gardening that could have thought of forming such an unsightly hollow into so beautiful an area.'

In her other hobby, hunting, Queen Anne took after her great-grandfather, James I. Like him she was happiest in the hunting-field, although not, at least as she grew older, in the saddle. Too clumsy and corpulent to ride, she followed the hunters in Windsor Great Park in a little chaise which she drove herself, 'furiously like Jehu,' wrote Swift in 1711 in his *Journal to Stella*, 'and is a mighty hunter, like Nimrod.' The Queen's love of horses inspired an interest in racing as well as hunting. She was the first royal owner and patron of Ascot race-course which she passed on to her successors, so that it is still, although non-profit-making, in the hands of the Royal Family today.

With her liking for a quiet country life and her lack of intelligent and stimulating conversation, it was no wonder that Anne's court was dull. The witty Swift, forced to attend one of her dreary 'drawing-rooms' found himself one of a company so small

that the Queen sent for us into her bedchamber, where we made our bows, and stood about twenty of us round the room, while she looked at us round with her fan in her mouth, and once a minute said about three words to some that were nearest her, and then was told dinner was ready, and went out . . .

Poor Anne, she was much happier gossiping about trivia with her women attendants than she was in the company of clever and critical men. Except for her husband, it was invariably women that she was closest to, in particular the domineering and temperamental Sarah, Duchess of Marlborough. Early in her reign, Anne would write four letters a day to this overbearing virago, addressing her as 'dear, dear Mrs Freeman' while she signed herself, 'Your poor, unfortunate, faithful [Mrs] Morley . . .' But thirty years' friendship turned sour as Sarah, perhaps sensing that her hold was loosening, became increasingly difficult and demanding. She would shout at the queen who, paralysed with fear, could scarcely answer her. When Anne tried to leave the room, Sarah, still shouting, would bar the door. In the spring of 1710 they had their last, terrible scene, when Sarah pushed her way into the queen's apartment, only to find Anne unmoved by her tears and taunting. After this, the two women never spoke to each other again. But the duchess still refused to give up her key of office as Mistress of the Robes until her long-suffering husband tried to wrest it from her and in a fit of rage she threw it on the floor. His 'wife', the Duke of Marlborough told a friend, often 'acted strangely, but there was no help for that, and a man must bear with a good deal to be quiet at home.'

Anne was now a widow. Two years before her husband had died in spite of her devoted nursing. She was genuinely upset although the Duchess of Marlborough commented maliciously that 'on that very day he died she ate three very large and hearty meals'. Sarah should have known the queen better. Nothing could ever stop her eating. In due course she became so fat that a special hoist was built to carry her up the stairs.

In her loneliness Anne turned to another woman friend for comfort. Abigail Masham, beak-nosed and highly intelligent, was a kinswoman and former protégé of the duchess's. She acted as secretary to the queen, helped her to compose her letters and was a tower of strength in the face of her ministers' violent quarrelling and bitter intrigues. Day after day the queen sat, bewildered and ignored at Council meetings, while Harley and Bolingbroke, her two chief ministers sniped at each other and hurled insults across the table. Without Abigail's support, Anne might well have collapsed sooner. As it was, she could not endure the strain indefinitely. In July 1714 after a particularly acrimonious session of the Council, the queen took to her bed, complaining of migraine. She had often said in the soft, gentle voice that was her chief asset, that all this quarrelling would cause her death. Now her prophecy came true. On 1 August she died, alone and friendless in the early hours of the morning. Out of earshot of her bed, her ministers squabbled right up to the end. Only her devoted Dr Arbuthnot, her own doctor who had nursed her devotedly, displayed any sympathy for her. 'Sleep,' he said afterwards, 'was never more welcome to a weary traveller.'

As befitted the last sovereign of the House of Stuart, Anne was buried in Henry VII's chapel at Westminster alongside Prince George, Charles II and both Mary and William. So fat had the queen become in the last, unhappy years of her reign, that her coffin, specially built for her, was almost square.

TOWN LIFE

To get a clear picture of London life in the latter part of the seventeenth century, we have to go back to 1660 and understand the feelings of relief and release which accompanied the restoration of the monarchy. After the comparative drabness of the Puritan years, Londoners hungered for colour. Taking its cue from the frivolous and fashion-conscious court, the city erupted in a riot of gaiety and extravagance. To Pepys, walking in Hyde Park in the summer of 1663, its citizens did not seem the same people. There was the queen, riding in a crimson petticoat and white-laced waistcoat, her hair dressed, as she was, 'à la negligence.' She looked, admitted Pepys grudgingly, 'in this dress . . . mighty pretty'. There were her ladies, 'fiddling with their hats and feathers, and changing and trying one another's by another's head, and laughing'. In the other parks the humbler Londoners strolled and gossipped in their own new finery and packed out the bear gardens and cockfights and refreshed themselves with 'certain trifling tarts, neats-tongues, salacious meats, and bad

Rhenish wine'. In Vauxhall Gardens, a contemporary wrote, there was music – 'here fiddles and there a harp, and here a Jew's trump, and here laughing, and there fine people walking'. Pepys was struck by the change. 'Lord! To see the difference of the times and but two years gone!' he wrote.

To an observer the clothes would have been the first and most apparent difference. Gone were the dull colours and prim high necks of the Puritan era. Now the fashion was to look *déshabillé*; to wear loose, unboned clothes, no head-dress, low necklines set off by strands of pearls. A taste for the exotic was the natural consequence of years of sobriety. The fashionable masked ladies who thronged newly opened playhouses like the Red Bull or Drury Lane, brought with them tiny West Indian boys as pages, richly dressed in the livery of their mistresses and chosen to complement the ladies' fair English skins.

The playhouses which had promptly re-opened by popular demand became a feature of Restoration life. Pepys was pleased to note their more elegant and refined atmosphere: wax candles to light the stage and clean stone instead of dirty rushes on the floor. Drury Lane could even boast a ragged orchestra of sorts with ten fiddlers, and the regular patronage of Charles II and his queen. The playhouses were the province of the Restoration playwrights – Congreve, Dryden, George Farquhar, Etherege, William Wycherley and Sir John Vanbrugh, who was also known as an architect. With the exception of Farquhar, they came from a rarified circle of metropolitan wits and gallants – Pope's 'mob of gentlemen who wrote with ease'. They performed to an audience drawn from the same fashionable upper classes and their plays reflected the mood of Charles II's court – cynical, bawdy, licentious, unashamedly secular after the previous years' excess of religion. Nothing was sacred, especially affairs of the heart. 'When your love's grown strong enough to make you bear being laughed at,' says a character in Etherege's *The Man of Mode*, 'I'll give you leave to trouble me with it: till then, pray, forbear, sir.' 'What indeed can any one mean, when he speaks of a fine gentleman,' asks a character in another play, 'but one who is qualified in conversation to please the best company of either sex?' No wonder the sober and worthy Dr Johnson felt it incumbent upon himself to attack 'the wits of Charles' in 1747:

> Themselves they studied, as they felt they writ;
> Intrigue was plot, obscenity was wit.
> Vice always found a sympathetic friend;
> They pleas'd their age, and did not aim to mend.

The first and last lines of this were right. In a way this Restoration generation was reacting against the idealism of the previous twenty years when men, Cavalier and Puritan, had been prepared to die for their beliefs. Restoration poetry like Restoration drama was not spiritually moving or lyrical or concerned with inner feelings. It was unashamedly matter-of-fact. Dryden, Charles II's Poet Laureate, wrote about the real world he saw around him, about the things we might read of today in a newspaper: people, places, politics, sex, drink, sport. Only, perhaps, when he talked about death, did he make mention of religion. And he had a healthy cynicism. Having composed a glowing ode to Oliver Cromwell, he felt perfectly able to greet the Restoration ecstatically in verse. The end result was very much the same as what has been said about Pepys's visits to the Restoration theatre: he never

42. Interior of a seventeenth-century coffee-house

once seemed to come away from it with what we today would call an idea.

The town wits and the journalists and writers mingled freely in what has been termed 'coffee-house society' after the 3000 coffee-houses (see plate 42) that had sprung up since Cromwell's time in London. Such places

> were very great enemies to diligence and industry, [complained a 1675 pamphlet], and 'have been the ruin of many serious and hopeful young gentlemen and tradesmen, who, before they frequented these places, were diligent students or shopkeepers, extraordinary husbands of their time as well as money . . . And for tea and chocolate, I know no good they do; only the places where they are sold are convenient for persons to meet in, sit half a day, and discourse with all companies that come in, of state-matters, talking of news, and broaching of lies . . .'

The *Spectator*, worried about these new exotic drinks, went even further. Writing of the forthcoming May festival, it said:

> I shall also advise my fair readers to be in a particular manner careful how they meddle with romances, novels, chocolates and the like inflamers, which I look on as very dangerous to be made use of during this great carnival.

Fortunately, the worried gentleman from the *Spectator* could reassure himself with the thought that at ten to fifteen shillings a pound, 'jocolatte' as Pepys called it, smacking his lips greedily, was far too expensive for all but the best-lined pockets. Tea was an even more exclusive commodity. At nearly fifty shillings a pound, it was only for the very rich indeed.

One of the leaders of coffee-house society and one who exemplified much that it stood for, was John Wilmot, Earl of Rochester (see plate 43). The son of an able and committed Cavalier general and an exceptionally pious Puritan lady, Rochester personified the post-war restoration generation. 'The Court not only debauched him; but made him an absolute Hobbist [aetheist],' complained Anthony à Wood, but this was an over-simplification. Rochester may have written bawdy verses and scurrilous lampoons but he also had a capacity for deeper and more

43. John Wilmot, Earl of Rochester

serious thought. Listen to him taking a clear view of a lifetime
of pointless pleasure-seeking and foreseeing an empty old age:

So when my days of Impotence approach,
  And I'm by Love and Wine's unlucky chance,
Driv'n from the pleasing Billows of Debauch,
  On the dull shore of lazy Temperance.

My pains at last some respite shall afford.
  While I behold the Battels you maintain:
When Fleets of Glasses sail around the Board,
  From whose Broad-Sides Volleys of Wit shall rain.

Anthony à Wood was right, however, in that Hobbes was the philosopher who, in standing for cool, analytical reason against 'the kingdom of darkness' (superstition and religion) was most likely to appeal to sceptical young men like Rochester. Thomas Hobbes was the arch-materialist. 'The universe is material,' he wrote, 'all that is real is material and what is not material is not real.' After publishing *Leviathan* in 1651 he was accused of aetheism and might well have come to grief in later years, had not Charles II stepped in to protect him and given him a pension of £100 a year. After 1660, he was a frequent visitor to Whitehall from his country estates in Malmesbury, Wiltshire. The king, vastly amused by the old man, left orders that he was to be admitted at any time.

The same spirit of secularism that motivated Hobbes also pervaded Restoration music. Before the Civil War, English music had carried on the Elizabethan tradition of many-voiced choral singing. Apart from church music, the main outlet for musicians like William Byrd or Wilbye was the madrigal or four-part song. Supposedly secular, these were composed on the same lines as church anthems and many of them were just as serious.

In many ways it was the taste of Charles II that brought about the revolution in English music. He brought back with him from France a liking for the light, airy music he had heard at the French court. One of his first actions was to reform the troupe of musicians attached to the Chapel Royal, which had been disbanded by the Puritans during the Commonwealth. In this he was probably trying to imitate King Louis of France who could boast an orchestra of twenty-four violins.

The violin, that 'upstart instrument', made its first appearance in England at the Restoration when it replaced the more cumbersome viol. It was ideally suited to the graceful, carefree music of the period and to the new fashion for using solo voices. Composer-in-Ordinary for the violin was the fiery Matthew Lock, a former Puritan pamphleteer whose music nevertheless echoed the atmosphere at Charles II's court. Lock had paved the way for the new French-influenced music, and for his young protégé, Henry Purcell, under whom it was to bear full fruit. Purcell was seventeen just before Lock was fifty but he was ably equipped to carry on and develop his predecessor's legacy. One of the greatest of our indigenous English composers, he wrote songs, masques, sonatas for strings and harpsichord and the first one-man English operas. He died young in 1695 but in his turn had paved the way for the great operatic compositions of the eighteenth century, especially those of George Friderick Handel.

Also in the spirit of the age was the foundation of the Royal Society, of which Charles II, with his interest in science, was the first patron. It took its motto from a phrase in the letters of the Latin poet, Horace: 'The words are the words of a master, but we are not forced to swear by them. Instead, we are to be borne wherever experiment drives us.' In the same vein but ahead of his time, Francis Bacon had said many years before: 'In speculations whoever begins with certainty will end with doubt; whoever begins with doubt and patiently entertains it for a while will end with certainty.' Thus, for the first time the old rigid beliefs of the Middle Ages were questioned. New techniques based on experiment brought fresh insight into the way the universe worked. For the first time men believed that there might be natural laws governing such things as the sky and the sea, and that they were not entirely at the mercy of an alternately angry and merciful God. The members of the Royal Society pledged themselves to examine the world around them in all its manifestations – plants, minerals, fish, fowl and animals. Not for them were the endless hours spent fruitlessly speculating on how, why or when God would punish the ungodly.

The first members of the Society were a uniquely versatile and

44. Samuel Pepys

gifted company. They included Samuel Pepys (see plate 44), known to his contemporaries, not, as he is to us, as a diarist but as an efficient and able naval administrator; John Evelyn who was a knowledgeable botanist and coin-collector; John Locke, philosopher, theologian and physician; Robert Hooke, a mathematician as well as a clergyman; Wren, who before he became an architect was a Professor of Astronomy; the poet, Dryden and the father of modern chemistry, Robert Boyle. In the early days the experiments they conducted were somewhat haphazard and purposeless

until, in 1684 Edmund Halley, the Senior Secretary of the Royal
Society, began consultations with the brilliant Cambridge mathe-
matician, Isaac Newton. From then on, inspired by Newton, the
Royal Society adopted a more scientific approach.

In many ways Isaac Newton embodies the seventeenth-century
scientific revolution. The principles laid down in his *Principia*
(published proudly under the auspices of the Royal Society) held
good for two hundred years. Born in 1642, he became Professor
of Mathematics at Cambridge when aged only twenty-seven and
went on to be President of the Royal Society for twenty-four
years. Besides his discovery of gravity, he wrote on optics and
built a telescope (see plate 45), formulated theories about tides

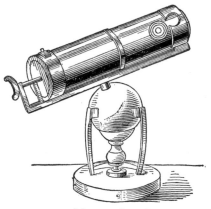

45. Newton's telescope

and mathematical equations and first made a case for the atomic
structure of light. His own brilliance made him unique among his
scientific contemporaries but he was not so unusual in the
methods he brought to bear on solving his problems. In his
questioning outlook he was in the mainstream of seventeenth-
century scientific thought.

Medicine, strangely enough, lagged behind the other scientific
disciplines. At the beginning of the eighteenth century Queen
Anne's physician was prescribing for her Spirit of Millipedes, a

euphonious name for ground-up creepy-crawlies in butter-balls.
Disease was held to be the result either of divine wrath or
superfluous 'humours' which could only be exorcized by subject-
ing the unfortunate patient to endless purges, blood-letting and
enemas. When Charles II was dying, for example, all his doctors
could suggest was cutting open a live pigeon and applying it to the
king's feet in an effort to draw out the disease. The one lone voice
in this wilderness of ignorance and superstition was that of
Thomas Sydenham whose patients included John Locke and
Robert Boyle. Carrying the new scientific methods into the field
of medicine he believed in bedside observation as a prelude to
the appropriate treatment of his patient. But he was a phenomen-
on indeed.

Few people, even in the late seventeenth century had any concept of hygiene. The City of London, for example, was still a very
unhealthy place. Samuel Pepys who lived in some style had a
long-standing feud with his neighbours whose privy regularly
overflowed, flooding his cellar. Mrs Pepys was only one of hundreds of Londoners who, when caught short in the street,
unconcernedly went 'in a corner [and] did her business'. Pepys
himself makes one mention of a bath in the nine years that he kept
his journal. His comment on the communal bathing at Bath (see
plate 46), was: 'Methinks it cannot be clean to go so many bodies
in the same water.' Not surprisingly his wife when she cut his
hair found 'that I am lousy, having found in my head and body
about twenty lice, little and great . . . being more than I have had,
I believe, these twenty years'.

Pepys was not alone in his unsanitary habits. Hygiene was not a
seventeenth-century virtue, and it was to be some time before any
but the greatest houses could boast of a bathroom. Illness was
blamed not on germs but on divine retribution. Many of the
direst prophecies of the Puritans were remembered and reinvoked
when plague broke out in 1665.

The 'great sweep of mortality', which, at its height, was to
claim 1000 lives a day in London, was treated at first as no more
serious than other random outbreaks of the years before. Indeed,
to the rich, it was something of a joke, visited fortunately almost

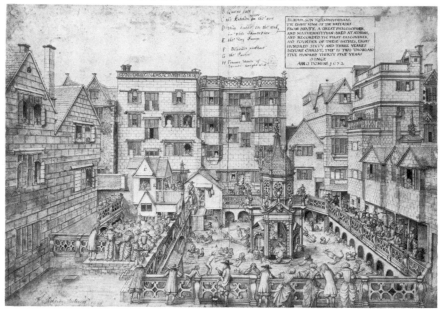

46. The King's and Queen's Baths at Bath

exclusively on the poor in their hovels. 'Tis plaguey news', jested Sir Ralph Verney heartlessly, 'that the plague has come to Southwark.' But before long, according to Sir Walter Besant, 'the mortality rising daily by leaps and bounds, the people sat down in their houses to die, or wandered disconsolately about the streets, marking the crosses on the doors with sinking hearts.'

Bubonic plague carried an almost certain death sentence, and a terrible one at that. Of those who fell victim to the initial fever, almost none recovered. Instead, they developed red blotches which swelled into buboes, and eventually burst. Medical science, as we have seen, was helpless in the face of the disease. Even the College of Physicians could only recommend applying onions to the tumour. It was left to the Londoners to cope with life in their doomed city as best they could.

Many of them fled altogether (see plate 47). Daniel Defoe was a child of five when the Great Plague broke out but later drew on his experiences in *Journal of the Plague Year*, which in view of his tender years has been called the first historical novel. He remem-

47. Fleeing from the Plague, 1665

bered seeing the Thames choked with small boats carrying frightened evacuees, some of them with their household goods tied up
in a bundle, others with only bales of straw to sleep on. The court
left Whitehall; the judges moved to Oxford; shops were closed
and shuttered, the streets empty and silent. Only the toll of
funeral bells broke the silence of what had become a ghost city,
that and the rumble of the corpse-wagons (see plate 48) circling
the city at night. 'Bring out your dead!'

At first the death toll was published weekly in 'Bills of Mortality' compiled by the parish clerks to whom all fatalities were
reported. But as the clerks and sextons perished one by one,
there was no one to keep any sort of record. We only have the

48. The Great Plague: a contemporary woodcut showing the
corpse-wagons leaving the city

49. The Great Plague: communal burial, as shown in a contemporary woodcut

rough estimates of such as Richard Baxter, a Nonconformist minister who estimated that over 100,000, mostly poor women and children, died. Mass graves had to be dug in which to dump the bodies (see plate 49). 'Now', mourned the Reverend Thomas Vincent, author of the eye-witness account, *God's Terrible Voice to the City*, 'the grave doth open its mouth without measure.'

Those who were left relied on a battery of spells, charms, secret recipes and holy medals to protect them. Some favoured strong drink to combat any possible infection (and perhaps soothe their nerves); others forbore to eat cherries, gooseberries and melon which were said to increase the risk of plague. The city authorities lit bonfires on street corners in the mistaken belief that heat might kill the disease.

In fact, the plague was at his height during the long, waterless summer months and it was when the first frost came that it began to abate. By November 1665, the rich who had fled were slowly returning, although it was routine to do as Pepys did and ask each day whether your friends were still alive. After Christmas even the court judged it safe to return.

Lord! [wrote Pepys] what staring to see a nobleman's coach come to town. And porters everywhere bow to us, and such begging of beggars! And a delightful thing is to see the towne full of people again as now it is; and shops begin to open.

After such a disaster had befallen London, none of its citizens can have dreamt that a blow of equal magnitude would fall the following year. The Great Fire of London (see colour plate 10), began as a small fire in a baker's shop in Pudding Lane. It was 3 a.m. on a hot autumn night and the flames spread quickly from house to house down the narrow street. The timbered houses were as dry as tinder after a summer with little rain. In a few hours the warehouses in Thames Street had been set alight and great quantities of tar, timber, coal, oil, rope and flax further fanned the blaze.

There was no stopping the fire now, certainly not with the pitiful contemporary water-engines which were nothing more than hand-operated squirts (see plate 50). And panic had begun to set in, as Samuel Pepys observed from his vantage point in a boat near London Bridge. He saw:

Everybody endeavouring to remove their goods, and flinging into the River or bringing them into lighters that lay off. Poor people staying in their houses as long as till the very fire touched them, and then running into boats or clambering from one pair of stair by the water-side to another. And among other things, the poor pigeons I perceive were loath to leave their houses, but hovered about the windows and balconies till they were some of them burned, their wings, and fell down.

It was Pepys who first informed King Charles II of the calamity. Efficient as ever, he recommended pulling down houses in the path of the fire. But when he went, armed with the king's blessing, to instruct the Lord Mayor to do this, he found the poor man distraught – 'like a man spent.' 'Lord! What can I do?' he was crying, 'I have been pulling down houses, but the fire overtakes us faster than we can do it!'

As night fell, Pepys saw the whole sky lit up by the fire. Sparks rained down on the unfortunate citizens and hot ash underfoot

50. Fire engine used in the Fire of London, 1666

burned through their shoes. Two days later the fire was still burning and anxiously Pepys returned home to salvage his belongings, including his precious diary. In a pit hastily dug in his garden he buried his papers and, strangely, a Parmesan cheese. He left that night, expecting never to see his house again.

But to his delight it was still standing when he returned at 7 a.m. and even better, the fire itself was dying down. In a few days it had destroyed the entire medieval city that Pepys knew and

loved, thirteen thousand houses in all. The great cathedral of St
Paul's was a gaunt, blackened ruin. In the heat the lead of its
roof had melted and run down the walls. Westminster Abbey,
Whitehall and the houses of the rich in the Strand had been saved
– Whitehall only to burn later in 1698 – but in the path of the fire
itself only a few stone churches survived.

It was this that led Charles II to formulate new rules for the
rebuilding of London. The 'lofty, lightsome, uniform and very
stately brick buildings' of the eighteenth century began to go up
in place of 'low dark wooden houses'. The streets were paved and
wider; proper sewers were built; businesses that made use of fire
were directed to certain 'safe' areas. London would never suffer
from plague or fire on such a scale again as it did in 1665 and 1666.

Six days after the fire ended, Christopher Wren presented his
plan for a splendid, new classical city to the king, a city of 'pomp
and regularity', a city which as Wren's son later said, could have
become 'the London of the world' (see plate 51). But there were
too many conflicting interests for his plan to be feasible: most
Londoners wanted to keep the right to build as they wished on
their own foundations. The city was rebuilt along the old medieval lines: although the streets were wider, they ran in the same
haphazard pattern, and you can still see this pattern in the City of

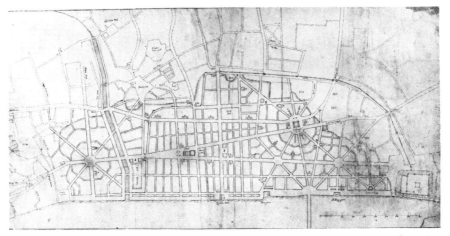

51. Wren's plan for a new, classical London, presented six days after the
fire in 1666

52. Wren's sign language for the deaf and dumb, capable of being 'learned in an hour'

London today. Nevertheless, Wren's plan was an important one in that it gained for him the chief architectural post in the land. When the old Surveyor-General, Sir John Denham died in 1669, he was promoted above more experienced architects – a sensible appointment because as Professor of Astronomy at Oxford, he was an accomplished mathematician and the new classical architecture required skill in measurement and calculation. Wren, indeed, was the Leonardo da Vinci of his time, capable of astonishing versatility. Interested in anatomy and physiology as well as astronomy, he experimented in injecting opium through a quill into the vein of a living dog. He also carried out a successful blood transfusion with a syringe, and invented a sign language for the deaf and dumb, capable of being 'learned in an hour' (see plate 52). But it was architecture that now began to occupy more and more of his time. As Surveyor-General he had the opportunity, and indeed the responsibility, of designing fifty-one city churches to replace the eighty-seven that had been burnt. The fire was his first and best patron.

The sites for the churches posed an enormous problem, being hemmed in by houses and either too small or awkwardly shaped. Wren changed this defect into an asset by giving each church an individual shape and style. Yet each also conformed to the graceful Renaissance traditions that he had inherited from an earlier Surveyor of the Works, Inigo Jones. With space at such a premium, he concentrated on ornamenting the spires, a Gothic feature which he invested with classical motifs (see plates 53, 54). The most splendid spire was that of St Mary-le-bow (see plate 55), built to house the famous Bow bells.

The last city church was finished in 1685 but by that time Wren had a larger problem to occupy him – the rebuilding of St Paul's Cathedral. It was to be 'a Design handsome and noble and suitable to the Ends of it, and to the Reputation of the City and the Nation', and Wren could 'take it for granted that Money will be had to accomplish it'. Money was never the problem. The problem was to get the king and the commissioners he had appointed to oversee the building to agree on a design. Wren had to submit several plans before there was a general consensus of opinion.

53, 54 and 55. The spires of Christ Church, Newgate Street, St Vedast and St Mary-le-Bow, Cheapside – three of the fifty-one new city churches designed by Wren after the fire

Fortunately, Wren was known for 'the sweet humanity of his disposition' and he went meekly back to the drawing-board even when they rejected his favourite design, the revolutionary 'Great

56. Wooden model of St Paul's, still on view in the Cathedral

Model' in the form of a Greek cross with a vast central circular
dome. The wooden model of it that Wren had built at a cost of
£500 can still be seen in St Paul's today (see plate 56). The last
design he drew was far more conventional, to please the conserva-
tive commissioners, but Wren was given liberty to 'make some
variations' as the building proceeded. He had to abandon the
Greek cross ground-plan in favour of a more usual cruciform
shape but he was able to keep his magnificent dome (see plate 57).
When in 1710 Wren's son placed the final stone on the cupola, the
gilded cross on top of it was an imposing 380 feet from the street
below.

The best craftsmen in England worked on the interior of St
Paul's, including Jean Tijou who was responsible for the iron-
work and Grinling Gibbons who carved the panelling and choir-
stalls. Sir James Thornhill, the celebrated artist, also painted
eight vast frescoes inside the dome, although Wren is not
supposed to have approved of them. More successful was Thornhill's Painted Hall in the additions Wren built at Greenwich, two
twin blocks also surmounted by domes. With the alterations to
Hampton Court and the building of the simple but dignified

57. St Paul's Cathedral: the south transept today

Chelsea Hospital for old soldiers (see plate 58), Wren's public commissions were almost complete. He died in 1723 at his house in St James's Street and was buried in the crypt of the cathedral he had created. On his monument was carved the appropriate epitaph, 'If you seek his monument, look around'.

58. Royal Hospital, Chelsea

From the smouldering ruins of the fire a new city had grown. A city described by Dryden in a poem:

> More great than human, now, and more August,
>   New deif'd she from her fires does rise:
> Her widening streets on new foundations trust,
>   And, opening, into larger parts she flies.

It was a fitting background to what has become known, from its preference for Latin literature, as the Augustan age, an age of elegance, and balance and urbanity, the age of Queen Anne. This was the age of prose in which men could conduct reasoned, logical arguments and forget the passions which had spawned so much strife in the generations before. Daniel Defoe, Richard Steele and Joseph Addison were the main exponents of this new prose style. All three founded newspapers which the coffee-house clientele readily bought. Among this talented group of literary men and

professional journalists were Jonathan Swift, the satirist, who had
already published some work although none as great as his future
masterpiece, *Gulliver's Travels*, and the poet, Alexander Pope.
The 'poet of professionals' Pope wrote for a closed and cultivated
circle. Learned references were lightly and colloquially dismissed;
the humour of his poem, *Rape of the Lock*, assumes a knowledge
of the classical epic form. From a precocious child Pope had
developed into a precocious poet, publishing the highly polished
Pastorals at the age of twenty-one. As a Roman Catholic he had
been debarred from university but a writer of his talent at large
in London could not fail to attract the friendship of such men as
Addison, Swift and Steele. Thus Pope became the poet who to us
represents the Augustan age.

Whereas in Charles II's time an army of scribes laboriously
transcribed 'newsletters' in London which were then passed from
hand to hand around the country, now with the founding of the
Tatler and later *Spectator*, the world of newspapers came into
being (see plate 59). In the opening months of Queen Anne's
reign the first daily newspaper, the *Daily Courant*, was published. By the end of her reign it had seven sister papers and there
was also a flourishing provincial press. The function of the newspapers was, according to Johnson, that 'to minds heated with
political contest they supplied cooler and more inoffensive
recollections.' This was the ethos behind the books of the philosopher of the age, John Locke. In 1690 his second *Treatise of Civil
Government* defined the rebalance of constitutional power and
upheld the subjects' rights. He argued his case on a basis of
common sense, reason and empiricism. When we read his clear,
reasoned arguments, we can see how far removed the Augustans
were from the days of the Civil War.

COUNTRY LIFE

The post-Restoration period saw a resumption of the country
house building begun tentatively in the days of Inigo Jones
but interrupted by the Civil War. In Charles II's time the two
greatest country house architects were Hugh May and Roger

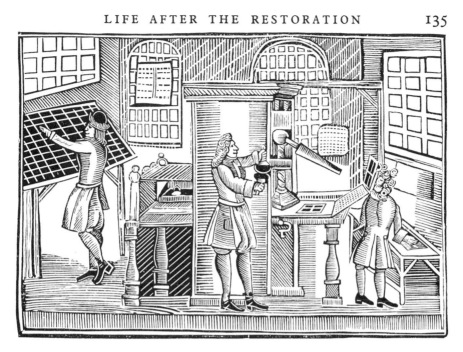

59. Printing works, 1710

Pratt who owed much to both Inigo Jones and Wren for their restrained classical façades (see plate 60). Wren himself was too occupied by public duties to undertake many commissions in the private field but he probably passed on work to his junior colleagues, Nicholas Hawksmoor and Sir John Vanbrugh. Together they were responsible for the architectural style which is known as English baroque.

Of the two, Vanbrugh was the more dominant, although completely untrained. Hawksmoor has never, in the eyes of posterity, fully emerged from his shadow. Yet Nicholas Hawksmoor was infinitely more experienced, having served his apprenticeship in Wren's office where he went as a clerk in 1679. He worked with Wren on, among other projects, St Paul's and Chelsea Hospital, but even during this period he had begun to develop an individual style – austere and sombre with a feeling for mass and monumentality (see colour plate 11).

Sir John Vanbrugh was a gentleman architect. He could be

60. Coleshill, Berkshire, by Roger Pratt

called a dilettante, were it not for his genius. Born into a family with county connections, he embarked first on a military career, and then joined the metropolitan wits of Charles II's time in writing for the stage. Of his eight or nine comedies the best known are *The Relapse* and *The Provok'd Wife*. Less well known is the fact that it was Vanbrugh who built the Queen's Theatre in the Haymarket, London, a theatrical venture to promote opera which only succeeded in losing him a great deal of money.

Vanbrugh came into architecture by the back door. Already on friendly terms with the artistic-minded among the nobility, he was asked by the Earl of Carlisle to replace the architect Talman at Castle Howard. Talman himself is a shadowy figure but his greatest achievement, the south front at Chatsworth House, is a landmark in seventeenth-century architecture. Built on an imposing and massive scale, it marked the very beginning of the movement towards baroque architecture.

Heaviness and a passion for ornamentation is what differentiates the baroque architects from classicists like Wren and Inigo Jones. Instead of flat façades they used colonnades and cupolas and porticos and pavilions. There is still symmetry but there is also a feeling of movement, illustrated in Vanbrugh's two

61. Blenheim Palace, Oxfordshire, by Sir John Vanbrugh

greatest houses, Castle Howard and Blenheim. Just to look at the
skyline of Castle Howard (see colour plate 12) is to understand
what this means. Blenheim too (see plate 61) is a great thrusting
mass of a building, heroic not domestic architecture. It succeeded
in its intent: to reflect the splendour of Marlborough's military
victories.

These are houses on a grand scale, well suited to what Defoe
called, when he toured England in the reign of Queen Anne, 'the
most flourishing and opulent country in the world'. To Celia
Fiennes who undertook her journeys around the turn of the
century, it was a pleasant and industrious kingdom. In provincial
towns like Newcastle and Exeter she noted approvingly the clean
streets and tidy, hard-working citizens. 'London in miniature' was
her comment on Newcastle. To her it was signal praise.

Celia Fiennes's confidence was not misplaced. The seventeenth
century generally, closed on an optimistic note. The poor were
still poor and the rich were still rich but at least there was wheaten
bread to eat and real wages at their highest level since Henry VI's
reign. More important, the long years of civil and religous
struggles had brought in their wake tolerance, peace and that
respect for the individual which is the hallmark of an Englishman.

꧅꧅꧅꧅꧅

BIBLIOGRAPHY

꧅꧅꧅꧅꧅

SOURCE MATERIAL

Defoe, Daniel. *A Journal of the Plague Year*. Edited by Louis A. Landa. Oxford University Press, London, 1972 and Penguin, Harmondsworth, 1970

D'Ewes, Sir Simonds. *The Journal of Sir Simonds D'Ewes*. Edited by Wallace Notestein. Humphrey Milford, Oxford University Press, London, 1942

Evelyn, John. *The Diary of John Evelyn*. Edited by Esmond S. de Beer. Oxford University Press, London, 1955

Fiennes, Celia. *The Journeys of Celia Fiennes*. Edited by Christopher Morris. Cresset Press, London, 1947

Hamilton, Anthony. *Memoirs of the Comte de Grammont*. Translated by Horace Walpole. Edited by David Hughes. Folio Society, London, 1965

Hutchinson, Lucy. *Memoirs of the Life of Colonel Hutchinson*. Everyman Library, Dent, London, 1965 and Everyman Paperbacks, Dent, London, 1972

Love, Harold (ed.). *The Penguin Book of Restoration Verse*. Penguin, Harmondsworth, 1968

Osborne, Dorothy. *Letters to Sir William Temple*. Edited by G. C. Moore Smith. Oxford University Press, London, 1928

Pepys, Samuel. *The Diary of Samuel Pepys*. Edited by Robert Latham and William Matthews. Bell, London, 1970–

WIDER READING

Ashley, Maurice. *England in the Seventeenth Century*. Pelican History of England Vol. 6. Penguin, Harmondsworth, 1970

——*Life in Stuart England*. Batsford, London, 1964

——*The Stuarts in Love*. Hodder and Stoughton, London, 1963

Bryant, Sir Arthur. *King Charles II*. Collins, London, 1960

——*Restoration England*. Collins, London, 1960

Butterfield, Herbert. *Origins of Modern Science*. Bell, London, 1970

Dutton, Ralph. *English Court Life from Henry VII to George II*. Batsford, London, 1963

Earle, Peter. *The Life and Times of James II*. Weidenfeld and Nicolson, London, 1972

Falkus, Christopher. *The Life and Times of Charles II*. Weidenfeld and Nicolson, London, 1972

Fraser, Antonia. *Cromwell: Our Chief of Men*. Weidenfeld and Nicolson, London, 1973

Ford, Boris (ed.). *From Donne to Marvell*. Pelican Guide to English Literature Vol. 3. Penguin, Harmondsworth, 1956

——*From Dryden to Johnson*. Pelican Guide to English Literature Vol. 4. Penguin, Harmondsworth, 1957

Hart, Roger. *English Life in the Seventeenth Century*. Wayland, London, 1970

Hibbert, Christopher. *The Life and Times of Charles I*. Weidenfeld and Nicolson, London, 1958

Hill, Christopher. *Puritanism and Revolution*. Secker and Warburg, London, 1958

——*Century of Revolution: 1603–1714*. Nelson, London, 1961

——*Intellectual Origins of the English Revolution*. Clarendon Press, Oxford, 1965

Hutchison, Harold. *Sir Christopher Wren*. Gollancz, London, 1976

Kenyon, J. P. *The Stuarts*. Wayland, London, 1970

Laslett, Peter. *The World We Have Lost*. Methuen University Paperbacks, London, 1971

Notestein, Wallace. *The English People on the Eve of Colonisation: 1603–1630*. Hamish Hamilton, London, 1934

Ogg, David. *England in the Reigns of James II and William III*. Oxford University Press, London, 1969

Ollard, Richard. *Pepys, a Biography*. Hodder and Stoughton, London, 1974

Summerson, John. *Architecture in Britain: 1530–1830*. Penguin, Harmondsworth, 1969

Trevelyan, G. M. *England under the Stuarts*. Methuen, London, 1904 and Methuen University Paperbacks, London, 1966

——*English Social History*. Longmans, London, 1944 and Penguin, Harmondsworth, 1970

Waterhouse, Ellis K. *Painting in Britain: 1530–1790*. Pelican History of Art. Penguin, Harmondsworth, 1969

Wedgwood, C. V. *Poetry and Politics under the Stuarts*. Cambridge University Press, Cambridge, 1960

Whinney, Margaret and Millar, Oliver. *English Art: 1625–1714*. Oxford University Press, London, 1957

Willey, Basil. *Seventeenth Century Background*. Chatto and Windus, London, 1934 and Penguin, Harmondsworth, 1972

Zee, Henri and Barbara Van de. *William and Mary*. Macmillan, London, 1973 and Pan, London, 1975

FICTION FOR THE SAME AGE GROUP

Bibby, Violet. *Many Waters*. Faber, London, 1974

Boston, Lucy M. *Children of Greene Knowe*. Faber, London, 1954

Burton, Hester. *Thomas*. Oxford University Press, London, 1969

——*Kate Rider*. Oxford University Press, London, 1974

Greaves, Margaret. *The Grandmother Stone*. Methuen, London, 1972

Harnett, Cynthia. *The Great House*. Methuen, London, 1941 and Penguin, Harmondsworth, 1968

Heyer, Georgette. *Royal Escape*. Heinemann, London, 1952 and Pan, London, 1970

Irwin, Margaret. *Proud Servant* and *Royal Flush*. Chatto, London, 1949 and Pan, London, 1971

——*Gay Galliard*. Chatto, London, 1956 and Pan, London, 1971

Marryat, Frederick. *The Children of the New Forest*. Collins, London, 1954 and many other editions

Softly, Barbara. *Place Mill*. Macmillan, London, 1962

——*Stone in a Pool*. Macmillan, London, 1964

Sutcliff, Rosemary. *Rider of the White Horse*. Hodder, London, 1967

——*Simon*. Oxford University Press (Oxford Children's Library), London, 1969

Vipont, Elfrida. *Children of the 'Mayflower'*. Heinemann, London, 1969

White, T. H. *Mistress Masham's Repose*. Cape, London, 1947 and Penguin, Harmondsworth, 1972

Willard, Barbara. *Grove of Green Holly*. Longman Young Books, London, 1967, and Puffin, Harmondsworth, 1969

——*Harrow and Harvest*. Kestrel, London, 1974.

INDEX

Addison, Joseph, 133, 134
  on Kensington Palace garden, 110
Anglicans, 74
  (*see also* Church of England, Protestants)
Anne of Denmark (James I's Queen), 14, 15,
  21, 23
  her love of masques, 22–3
Anne, Queen of England (reigned 1702–14),
  98, 105, plate 41, 108–12, 120
  'Augustan Age', 133–4
  love of horses, 110
  poor patron of the arts, 109–10
Anti-clericalism, 41–2
Arbuthnot, Dr (Queen Anne's doctor), 112
Architecture, 19, 20, 28–9, 90, 102–3, 104–5,
  109, 127–32, 134–7
  Tudor, 19–20, 59, 103
  (*see also* Jones, Hawksmoor, Vanbrugh,
  Wren)
Army, Parliamentary, 69, plate 26, 85
  Cromwell's New Model Army, 78
  dissolved Parliament, 85
Art
  decorative, 20, 21, 30–1, 91, 96, 103, 109
  Delft ware, 103
  destruction by Cromwell's men, 20
  flourished under Charles I and II, 19–24,
  89
  furniture, 31, 40, 44, 109
  Stuart gentry ignorant of, 31–3
  under Queen Anne, 109
  (*see also* Architecture, Masques, Music,
  Painting)
Assheton, Nicholas, 33
Aubrey, John, 72
'Augustan Age', 133–4
Austen, Jane, 36

Bacon, Francis, 118
Bath, 121, plate 46
Baxter, Richard, 61, 124
Bentinck, Lord William (Earl of Portland),
  102
Berkeley, Lord, 29–30
Bernini, G. L. (Italian sculptor), 17, 21
  on Charles I, 18
Besant, Sir Walter
  on plague, 122
Bible, Authorized Version of, 40
Bloodless Revolution (1688), 98–9
Bolingbroke, Henry, 111
Boyle, Robert, 119, 121

Bradford, William (Puritan leader), 64–7
Breton, Nicholas, 46
  on clergy, 37
  on merchants, 53
Brome, Richard
  The Sparagus Garden, 44
Brown, Lancelot ('Capability Brown'), 36
Buccleuch, Earl of
  his bed, 30
Buckingham, Duke of, *see* Villiers
Bunyan, John, 61
  The Pilgrim's Progress, 61
Burbage, Richard (actor), 56
Burnet, Gilbert (Bishop)
  on William and Mary, 99, 100, 102, 107
Burton, Henry (Puritan), 61

Calvinists, 70–1
Carr, Robert (favourite of James I), 15–16
Cary, Lucius (Viscount Falkland), 71
Castlemaine, Barbara (mistress of Charles II),
  92, plate 35, 93
Catherine of Braganza (Charles II's Queen),
  92–3, colour plate 9
Catholics, 10, 96, 101
  'popery' and anti-catholic feeling, 24, 60,
  64, 70, 93–4, 96, 97–8, 101
Charles I (reigned 1625–49), 16–24, plate 2, 25,
  colour plate 6
  and Parliament, 63–4
  and the Puritans, 60, 63
  as martyr, 80
  causes of downfall, 18, 20, 23
  character, 16–19
  death, 76–7, plate 28, 87, plate 33
  his wife, *see* Henrietta Maria
  'Museum Minervae', 21
  palaces, 19, 21–2
  patron of the arts, 19–24
  unpopularity, 23–4
  (*see also* Civil War)
Charles II (reigned 1660–85), 86–94, 97, 100,
  121, 125, colour plate 8
  court, 88–9, 113
  his mistresses, 92, plate 35
  his wife, *see* Catherine of Braganza
  love of things French, 88–9, 117–18
  patron of the arts and sciences, 89–91, 113,
  117–20
  popularity, 86–8, 89–91
  Restoration (q.v.), 85, 86–8
Charlotte, Countess of Derby, 72–3

Christian IV of Denmark, 14
Church of England, 10
    abuses in, 37–8, 40, 60
    reform demanded, 40
    rift with Puritans, 40–2
    (see also Clergy)
Churchill, Sarah (Duchess of Marlborough),
    100, 105, 109, 111
    (see also Marlborough, Duke of)
Civil War (1640–9), 9, 25, 70–7
    City merchants in, 53
    decisive battles, 74, 78–9, plate 29
    yeomen in, 46
City merchants, 52–4, plate 19
    take Puritan side in Civil War, 53–4, 87
    (see also London)
Clarendon, Edward (historian), 57, 58, 71
Clergy, 37–42, plate 12
    their poverty, 37, 40
Coffee-houses, 101, plate 42, 115, 133
    first one opened, 83
Commonwealth (1649–60), 78–85
    life under, 81–5, plate 30
Congreve, William, 113
Cooper, Samuel, 84
Coriat, Thomas
    on London playhouses, 54
Cork, Lord, 36
Correggio, 21
Covenanters (Scottish), 71, 79
Cowley, Abraham (poet), 74
    on Charles I's death, 76
Cranfield, Lionel, 52
Crashaw, Richard, 39
Cromwell, Oliver, plate 27, 82–3, 85
    broke up Charles I's art collection, 20
    condemned Levellers, 68
    his army, 61
    in Civil War, 74, 78
    New Model Army, 78

Defoe, Daniel, 133, 137
    Journal of the Plague Year, 122–3
    on Queen Anne, 109
    Tour of Great Britain, 103
Dekker, Thomas
    on London, 51
    Shoemaker's Holiday, 53
Denham, Sir John (Charles II's Surveyor
    General), 90, 129
Divine right of kings, 17, 23, 64, 94
Donne, John, 28, 56, 57, 58
    his poetry, 57
Dryden, John, 113, 114, 119
    on London, 133

Eachard, John, 40
Earle, John
    Microcosmographie, 57
    on taverns, 58
East India Company, 53, 103
Eliot, Sir John, 83
Elizabeth I (reigned 1558–1603), 10, 12, 14
Elizabeth, daughter of James I, 17
Etherege, Sir George
    The Man of Mode, 113
Evelyn, John, 33, plate 9, 86, 91, 98, 103, 117
    on restoration of Whitehall, 89
    on stench of London, 58–9
    shocked by Charles II, 93
    shocked by James II, 96
Eyre, Adam, 43, 44, 46

Fairfax, Lord Thomas (General), 76

Farquhar, George, 113
Fielding, Henry
    Tom Jones, 28
Fiennes, Celia (traveller), 86, 105, 109, 137
Fleetwood, Charles (Roundhead), 79
Frederick V, Elector Palatine, 17
Fuller, Thomas, 58, 74–5

George I (reigned 1714–27), 108
    unappreciative of arts, 109
George, Prince of Denmark (Queen Anne's
    husband), 108–9, 111
Gibbons, Grinling, 91, 96, 103, 131
Giorgione, 21
Gloucester, Duke of (son of Queen Anne), 105,
    plate 41
Grammont, Comte de, 86
    on James I, 94
Greenwich Palace (Greenwich Hospital), 21,
    90–1, 106, plate 40, 131
Gwyn, Eleanor ('Nell' Gwynne – mistress of
    Charles II), 92, plate 35, 93

Halley, Edmund, 120
Hampden, John, 27, 83
Hampton Court Conference (1604), 40
Hampton Court Palace, 21, 102–3, plate 39,
    105, 106–7, 131
Handel, George Frederick, 118
Hardwick Hall
    bed (Lapierre Canopy), colour plate 5
Harington, Sir John, 14
    inventor of water-closet, 14, 31
    The Englishman's Doctor, 31
Harley, R., 111
Hawksmoor, Nicholas, 135, colour plate 11
    on Queen Mary, 104
Henrietta Maria (Charles I's Queen), 21, 22,
    23–4, 93, colour plate 4
    love of masques, 23–4
    'papist', 24, 93
Henry VIII (reigned 1509–47), 9–10
    dissolution of monasteries, 37
Henry, Prince (first son of James I), 16–17
Herbert, George, 28, plate 8, 38–9
Herrick, Robert, 57
Hobbes, Thomas, 28, 117
    'Hobbism', 115, 117
    Leviathan, 117
Holyrood Palace, 13
Honeywell, William, 46
Hooke, Robert (mathematician), 119
Horace (Latin poet), 118
Houckgeest, Joachim
    painted Charles I, 52, colour plate 6
House of Commons, 41–2, 85, plate 32
    (see also Parliament)
Howard, Thomas, Earl of Arundel, 33
Hutchinson, John, 82
Hutchinson, Lucy, 18, 73, 83
Hyde, Anne (first wife of James II), 98, 108
Hyde, Edward (Earl of Clarendon), 70, 87, 98

Indemnity, Act of, 87

James I (James VI of Scotland reigned 1603–
    25), 11–16, 18, 23, 24, colour plate 1
    character, 11–12, 14, 15–16
    court, 12–16, 20
    favourites, 15–16
    his wife, see Anne of Denmark
    household, 13
    love of hunting, 14, 101, 110
    on London, 50

on Parliament, 27
Trew Law of Free Monarchies, 23
James II (reigned 1685–8), 94–9, 101, 108
  court, 96
  fled to France, 78, 99
  his wife, *see* Mary of Modena
  'papist', 93–4, 97–8, 108
  unpopularity, 94, 95–9, 108
Jefferies, Mrs, 73
Jeffreys, George ('Judge Jeffreys'), 97
Johnson, Samuel, 114, 134
Jones, Inigo, 19, 20, 21, plates 5 and 6, 33,
    plate 40, 129, 135
  and Ben Jonson, 23–4
  Banqueting House, Whitehall, 19, plates 3
    and 17, colour plate 3
  piazza at Covent Garden, plate 4 (p 20)
  Queen's Chapel at St James's, 24
Jonson, Ben, 14, 23–4, 28, 49, 56, 58
  and Inigo Jones, 23–4
  as talker, 58
  Chloridia, 23
  Cynthia's Revels, 52
  on Puritans, 81
  Poetaster, 54
  The Magnetick Lady, 40
  The Malcontents, 54
  The Masque of Queens, 23

Kensington Palace, 107, 109–10
  bought by William and Mary, 105
Keppel, Arnoud van (Earl of Albemarle), 102
Kéroualle, Louise de (mistress of Charles II),
    92, plate 35
Kneller, Sir Godfrey, 109–10
  painted James II, plate 36 (p 95)
  portraits of Kit-Kat Club, 110

Laud, William (Archbishop), 41, 60–1, plate
    12, 64, 70–1
  enemy of Puritans, 41, 60
Lauderdale, Duke of, 30
  his bed, 30
  on James II, 94
Lawson, George, 63
Lely, Sir Peter, 89, 109
Levellers, the, 68
Life in Stuart England
  beds, 30–1, colour plate 5
  country life, 25–47, plates 13 and 14, 134–7
  courtly life, 12–16, 20, 52, plate 18, 54, 63
  domestic life, 29–33, 121
  dress, 14, 23, 31, 52, 83, plate 31, 89, 112–13
  gentry, 25–36, plates 7, 10 and 11, 38, 41–2,
    50, 63, 88
  medicine and hygiene, 120–1, 122 (*see also*
    Plague)
  social classes ('gentle' and 'simple'), 25–7
  town life, 48–59, plate 15
  yeomen and farm workers, 42–7, 61, plate 22
Lilburne, John (Puritan), 61, 68
Lilly, William (astrologer), 83
Literature, 28, 56–8, 86, 133–4
  religious poetry, 38–9
Lock, Matthew, 118
Locke, John, 119, 121
  Treatise of Civil Government, 134
London, 49–59, plate 16
  and Civil War, 72
  City, 50, 52, 59, 121
  Great Fire (1666), 125–7, plate 50, colour
    plate 10
  Great Plague (1665), 59, 121–5, plates 47–9
  Inns of Court, 57–8

playhouses, 54–6, plate 21
rebuilt after Great Fire, 127–33
rejoices at Restoration, 86–7
  (*see also* City merchants)
Louis XIV of France, 88–9, 117
Lovelace, Richard, 33, 80
Lucy, Countess of Bedford, 56
Lupton, Donald
  on playwrights, 54

Mantegna, 21
Markham, Gervase
  The English Huswife, 35
Marlborough, Duke of, 105, 111, 137
  his wife, *see* Churchill, Sarah
Mary, Queen of England (1689–94), 98–106,
    plate 37
  grew up Protestant, 98
  death, 105–6
  interest in the arts, 103–5
  married William of Orange, 98
Mary of Modena (James II's Queen), 93, 96,
    98–9
Marot, Daniel (Dutch designer), 103
Marvell, Andrew
  on Charles I's death, 76–7
  on Civil War, 71–2
Masham, Abigail (friend of Queen Anne), 111–
    12
Masques, 22–4, plate 6, 82, 118
  Chloridia, 23
May, Hugh, 134–5
Michelangelo, 32
Middleton, Thomas, 54
  The Roaring Girl, 51
Mildmay, Sir Humphrey
  his London pleasures, 52
Millenary Petition (1603), 40
Milton, John, 10, 57, 71–2, 83, 85
  on Church of England, 60
  Paradise Lost, 48
  Samson Agonistes, 85
Monmouth, Duke of, 97
  Battle of Sedgemoor, 97
Music, 47, 82–3, 117–18
  (*see also* Masques)
Mytens, Daniel (Dutch artist), 21

Newspapers, 134, plate 59
  Daily Courant, 134
  Tatler, 134
  (*see also Spectator*)
Newton, Sir Isaac, 10, 120
  his telescope, 120, plate 45
Normanton, idle Rector of, 37
Nottingham, Lord, 105

Osborne, Dorothy, 72, 73, 80
  on country life, 46
  on life under Protectorate, 83–5

Painting, 19–21, 31–2, 89, 91, 109–10
Parkinson, John, 35
Parliament, 9, 27, 50, 85
  Charles I, 63–4
  Puritans, 63–4
  William and Mary, 105, 106
  (*see also* Army, Civil War)
Pembroke, Earl of, 20
Pepys, Samuel, 10, 86, 112–13, 115, 119, plate
    44, 121, 124–6
  his wife, 121
Philosophical Society
  supported by Charles II, 91

Plague, 59
  The Great Plague (1665), 59, 121–5, plates
    47–9
Pope, Alexander, 110, 113, 134
  Rape of the Lock, 134
  The Dunciad, 59
'Popery', *see under* Catholics
Pratt, Roger, 134–5, plate 60
Pride, Thomas (Roundhead), 79
Protestants, 10, 96, 100
  (*see also* Church of England, Anglicans)
Protestant Succession, 98–9, 108
Prynne, William (Puritan), 61
Purcell, Henry, 118
Puritans and puritanism, 10, 27, 36, 60–9,
    plate 83, 89
  and Parliament, 63–4
  and the New World, 64–7, plates 23–5,
    colour plate 7
  education, 61, plate 23
  rift with Church hierarchy, 40–2, plate 12
Pym, John (Puritan), 71

Raphael, 21, 32–3, 89
Restoration, the (1660), 85, 86–8
  cause of rejoicing, 86–7, 112
  drama, 113–15
  music, 117–18
  poetry, 114
Richardson, Lord Chief Justice, 41
Richelieu, Cardinal, 42
Richmond Palace, 21, 96
Roundheads, 73, 78–9
  (*see also* Civil War)
Rowlands, Richard
  on dress, 14
Royal Society, the, 91, 118–20
Royalists, 72–3, 78–9
  (*see also* Civil War)
Rubens, Peter Paul, 19, colour plate 3
  painting of James I, 23
Rupert, Prince (nephew of Charles I), 78

Saint Albans, Duke of, 96
Saint Paul, 81
Saint Paul's Cathedral
  burnt in Great Fire, 127
  rebuilt, 129–31, plates 56 and 57
Salisbury, Lord, 14
Science, 91, 118–21
  (*see also* Charles II, Royal Society)
Scuderi, Madeleine de, 84
Shakespeare, William, 10, 28, 54, 55–6, plate 21
  as talker, 58
  on English yeomen, 42
Ship Money, 64
Sophia, Electress of Hanover (mother of George
    I), 108
Spectator, 115, 134
Steele, Richard, 133, 134
Stettin, Duke of, 47
Stow, John, 57
Strafford, *see* Wentworth
Stuarts, the, 9
  belief in divine right of kings, 17, 23, 64,
    94
  (*see also* Anne, Charles I and II, James I and
    II)
Suckling, John, 58
Swift, Jonathan, 110, 134
  Journal to Stella, 110
Sydenham, Thomas (doctor), 121

Talman, G. (architect), 136
Taylor, John
  An Arrant Thief, 51
Theatre, 54–5, 113–14
Thornhill, Sir James, 131
Tintoretto, 21
Titian, 21, 89
Tijou, Jean, 131
Tusser, Thomas, 45

Vanbrugh, Sir John, 113, 135–7, plate 61,
    colour plate 12
Van Dyck, Sir Anthony, 21, 89
  painted Charles I, plate 2 (p 17)
  painted Henrietta Maria, 21, colour plate 4
Vaughan, Henry, 39
Verney, Sir Ralph
  on plague, 122
Verrio, Antonio (Italian painter), 91, 96, 103
Villiers, Elizabeth (mistress of William III), 101
Villiers, George (Duke of Buckingham), colour
    plate 2
  favourite of Charles I, 18, 23
  favourite of James I, 16
Vincent, Thomas
  on plague, 124
Visscher, Cornelis
  map of London, plate 16 (p 50)

Walter, Lucy (mistress of Charles II), 92,
    plate 35, 97
Walton, Izaak
  friend of George Herbert, 38–9
Webb, John (architect), 90–1, plate 40
  worked with Inigo Jones, 20
Wentworth, Thomas (Earl of Strafford), 64, 71
  executed, 71
Whalley, Richard
  on country gentry, 27–8
Whitehall, royal palace of, 12–13, 19, plate 3,
    33, plates 5 and 17, 50, 96, 100, colour
    plates 3 and 6
  after Restoration, 88, 89
  destroyed by fire, 50, 105, 127
  disliked by William III, 102
Whitgift, Archbishop, 37
Wilkins, John, 68
William of Orange, William III (1689–1702),
    98–107, plate 37
  his wars, 101
  resented by the English, 102
Wilmot, John (Earl of Rochester), 115–17,
    plate 42
Wilson, Thomas, 48
Windsor Castle, 21, 91, 109
Winstanley, Gerrard, 68
Wolsey, Cardinal, 42, 102
Women, life of, 33–36, 43, 44–5
Wood, Anthony à
  on Rochester, 115–17
Wren, Christopher, 10, 90, plate 34, 91, 96, 104,
    119, 128–32, 135
  Chelsea Hospital, 132, plate 58, 135
  design of churches, 129, plates 53–5
  Greenwich Hospital, 106, plate 40, 131
  Hampton Court, 102–3, plate 39, 106, 109,
    131
  plan for rebuilding London after Great Fire,
    127, plate 51
  Saint Paul's Cathedral, 10, 129–31, plates 56
    and 57, 135
  sign-language, 129, plate 52
Wycherley, William, 113